What people

Generation Panic

Generation Panic is an ideal guide and companion for anyone struggling under the weight of a demanding, fast-paced life. Agi expertly targets a group of people who may not otherwise seek help, leading them to better mental health with straight-forward strategies that really work. A must read for anyone suffering with anxiety.
– Alice Mackintosh, Registered Nutritional Therapist

In *Generation Panic,* author Agi Heale offers accessible, easy-to-use techniques for managing anxiety sourced from her own experience. If you struggle with anxiety and long to be able to embrace a life of ease this book is for you. It is brimming with ideas and practical strategies to help you create sustainable change and set yourself free.
– Karen Kimsey-House, co-author of *Co-Active Coaching* and co-founder of The Co-Active Training Institute

Since I suffered two major anxiety-driven depressive episodes in my thirties, I have discovered my own ways to stay calm and well. My life would have been much easier if only Agi Heale's brilliant book had been around when I was unwell. I have learnt much from *Generation Panic*: what anxiety is, and fresh psychological and physical strategies to defeat its grip. Were I to wobble again, I have found a book I can return to: a companion to remember things that can help me feel confident and strong and something I would highly recommend to others.
– Rachel Kelly, writer and mental health campaigner and author of *Sunday Times* Top Ten Bestseller *Black Rainbow: How words healed me – my journey through depression*

This book is a gem. It is the fusion of personal experience of anxiety, of helping others cope with their fears and of keen reading of the relevant research. It is accessible, practical and embodies the empathy that is truly therapeutic.
– Dr David Pendleton, Professor in Leadership, Henley Business School

Don't panic – there's a lot you can do to regain control. I'm delighted that Agi Heale has gathered so many practical tools together. These have been tested in her moments of need and they can be used by all of us. I strongly recommend that you see what works for you and those you care for.
– Ian McDermott, founder of International Teaching Seminars (www.itsnlp.com)

I related so much to Agi's GP story, having been in a similar place myself. I loved the easy tips and strategies that I felt I could implement immediately upon starting *Generation Panic*. By sharing her own personal experiences throughout the chapters, it reminds readers that they are not alone in their anxieties, stress and panic. This book is going to be a great help to a lot of people.
– Charlie Watson, RD, author of *Cook, Eat, Run*

In my 20 years as an Executive Coach, I can attest to the widespread impact anxiety has on people at all levels of modern organisations. In this wonderful book, Agi has not only been incredibly brave and vulnerable in sharing her own experiences with anxiety, but has provided a menu of simple, pragmatic, and very effective tools and techniques that can be readily applied to help overcome its debilitating impacts.
– Rob Balmer, Managing Director – Executive Central Group

Generation Panic

Simple & Empowering Techniques to Combat Anxiety

Generation Panic

Simple & Empowering Techniques
to Combat Anxiety

Agi Heale, CPCC, PCC & Certified
NLP Practitioner

BOOKS

Winchester, UK
Washington, USA

JOHN HUNT PUBLISHING

First published by O-Books, 2021
O-Books is an imprint of John Hunt Publishing Ltd., 3 East St., Alresford,
Hampshire SO24 9EE, UK
office@jhpbooks.com
www.johnhuntpublishing.com
www.o-books.com

For distributor details and how to order please visit the 'Ordering' section on our website.

Text copyright: Agi Heale 2020
Cover design: David Provolo
Illustrations: Millie Baring (www.millustrations.co.uk)

Editor: Christina Roth

ISBN: 978 1 78904 515 4
978 1 78904 516 1 (ebook)
Library of Congress Control Number: 2019952954

Design: Stuart Davies
www.stuartdaviesfineart.com

Disclaimer: I am not an expert in this field. I am not a neuroscientist, psychologist, therapist,
or doctor. I have written this book based on my own experience and from my own perspective.
It is not intended to replace any professional medical or psychological advice. Any material
from this book is at the reader's discretion. Please consult an expert for any advice.

UK: Printed and bound by CPI Group (UK) Ltd, Croydon, CR0 4YY
Printed in North America by CPI GPS partners

We operate a distinctive and ethical publishing philosophy in
all areas of our business, from our global network of authors to
production and worldwide distribution.

Contents

For Lola

And future generations.

May you be kind, happy and free of anxiety.

Author's Note on Illustrations

I'm pleased to introduce you to George and Polly, little characters that I have grown immensely fond of. Their egg-like and endearing quality represents the fragility and likability of Generation Panic.

I hope you enjoy them joining us in this book, and on your journey with anxiety, as much as I do.

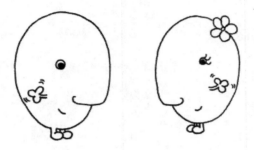

Introduction

You have brains in your head. You have feet in your shoes. You can steer yourself any direction you choose. You're on your own. And you know what you know. And YOU are the one who'll decide where to go.

– Dr. Seuss, *Oh, The Places You'll Go!*

Who Are Generation Panic?

I am part of Generation Panic. No question about it. And if you've picked up this book, I'll bet you are too.

Generation Panic, or GP'ers, is what I call the group of people in their twenties and thirties who battle with anxiety on some level. They are often strong, brilliant, ambitious people, but they have a big dollop of insecurity that makes them wobble at certain moments of their lives. GP'ers are high-potential professionals and rising talent who expect a great deal of themselves and hold themselves to the highest standards. Moreover, the grass always seems greener when they compare themselves to their contemporaries who seem to be doing well. As a consequence, they feel like they are failing miserably.

During these years, GP'ers experience a lot of change. They can be anywhere from single with absolutely no desire for a relationship to settled down with kids and a family. GP'ers might not be working or might be starting out in new careers, or they could be very established and senior in their work. Within that time frame, high-achieving individuals in their twenties and thirties will feel ongoing pressure to look good, keep up with social media, date if they're single, be healthy, get married, excel in a job, start a family, socialise at work, see friends and catch up with family, get on the property ladder – all whilst looking like everything is under control and ensuring they don't mess up. It's never-ending as we try to 'keep up'. The one constant that GP'ers can be sure of is anxiety.

My Generation Panic Story

As a GP'er, I was – and continue to be – incredibly ambitious. I spent years feeling like I needed to prove who I was to, not only myself, but also everyone around me. At the time of my most crippling panic attacks and anxiety, I was doing far too much. At my job in Financial Services recruitment, I had progressed quickly to levels of significant responsibility and gained success (at least one version of it). Alongside a demanding job, I was also desperate to maintain friendships and other relationships. Adding to it all, I had the pressure of arranging my wedding. I felt stuck on the hamster wheel but was terrified of falling off. I was determined to show people that I could handle it all.

In the end, my body reacted. It was doing things on its own accord, and I couldn't regulate myself. Since I had always been in control, this was a scary experience.

I felt totally lost, disconnected, exhausted and desperate to feel more in control. And the icing on the cake was that I was too proud to admit that anything was wrong or that I needed help. I knew continuing with the way things were wasn't right, but I didn't know how to change or even where to start.

Over the next few months, I was desperate to maintain my façade that everything was under control. I searched for anything that could help me feel positive, happier and more confident – essentially, like myself again. I slowly tested a whole range of things to help me, and I learnt a great deal in the process.

I wish at that time that I had been given a 'one-stop-shop' book that gave me all the information I needed to get back on track. My ability to concentrate, take in new information and implement it was limited, so I was desperate for something I could just pick up, grab a snippet from, try it out and then put it back down.

I have gleaned and nurtured all of what follows from my personal experience and my work with clients as a certified professional coach. In short, I wrote this book for myself as a reminder that if I ever 'wobble' and feel on edge, I can jump into a chapter and remind myself of everything I already know. I can get back on track, and quickly. It is one place I can return to again and again, even if I get derailed with challenges, to remember all the things that have helped me feel more confident, calmer and stronger – more myself and back to centre. My hope is that this distilled information will benefit you as powerfully as it has for me and those I've worked with.

What This Book Can Do for You

Generation Panic is aimed at busy people who suffer from anxiety and want a helpful reference to pick up and put down with ease. In reading this book, you will get tools to reduce your anxiety and panic and ultimately change the way you live. With bite-size, short chapters, you can dip in and out, reading as little or as much as you can or want. Maybe just a chapter today, or one quick technique to boost yourself before an upcoming meeting.

You might begin by flicking through and just touching on the areas that speak to you. In time, I strongly urge you to invest in yourself and read the whole book diligently, trying out all the different tips and tricks. Take the time to pause and reflect, highlight sections, write notes and find what works best for you. Make sure it is easy for you to refer back to in the future. In between chapters, take a breather to consider what relates to you and to think about how you want to tweak things. As you return to *Generation Panic* over the weeks and months, you can lock in the learning by trying out new things to strengthen your toolkit.

The more chapters you read to build your knowledge, and the more you apply what you've learned, the stronger you will feel in the face of anxiety. Investing your time in these new habits is like working on a new muscle in the gym. Often after the first few sessions, you feel great and as though you are making good progress. However, if you stopped there, then you would revert back, and the muscle would stop growing. Instead, you need to continue and commit to becoming strong and building the muscle up.

Like me, you may struggle at times to remember these techniques and implement them into your daily life, and anxiety will get back into the driving seat. If that happens, just go back to the basics; take a deep breath and reconnect with all the resources you have at your fingertips.

With all of life's ever-changing uncertainties, you cannot control what happens to you each day, but you can control your reactions. This book gives you a new box of tools to help you get through anything. How you adapt and the resources you use will impact how quickly and well you will fare despite the inevitable blips in the road. This book shows you that it is possible to connect back to your positive self and feel confident, unstoppable and energised again.

To Round Up

I hope you find this book useful. If it helps you feel even a little calmer and have a better relationship with anxiety, then it will have been worth it for me.

I hope we can begin to talk openly about anxiety and raise awareness about panic attacks. In doing so, Generation Panic can be a healthier, happier and more aware generation. My dream is for Generation Panic to become Generation Awesome. I believe it can happen with these tools, and I hope that you share the same vision.

A final pointer: change happens over time, so start now. The longer you put it off, the harder it becomes. The heavy weight you carry around with you every day just gets heavier. One small tweak, one small tip can set the wheels in motion and help alleviate that weight. As Lao Tzu said, 'A journey of a thousand miles begins with a single step.'

For now, enjoy and have fun! And don't forget, be kind to yourself.

Agi

P.S. Keep in Touch

Please do keep the conversation going at www.generationpanic. com. I would love to hear what you've enjoyed learning or any other ideas you use for your anxiety. You can also follow me on social media (using the handle of generationpanic), or Instagram under @generationpanic or #generationpanic.

I look forward to hearing from you!

Happy reading.

1. In the Panic

Our greatest glory is, not in never falling, but in rising every time we fall.
– Oliver Goldsmith

1.1 Fight or Flight
1.2 Breathe Deep
1.3 The Heartbeat Tapper
1.4 Your Body Speaks
1.5 Cue Cards

1.1 Fight or Flight

Storms make the oak grow deeper roots.
– George Herbert

Snapshot

The fight-or-flight response is our reaction to danger. It helps us to react to life-threatening scenarios quickly, effectively and without thought. As explained in 'Understanding the Stress Response' by Harvard Health Publishing, 'when someone experiences a stressful event, the amygdala, an area of the brain that contributes to emotional processing, sends a distress signal to the hypothalamus. This area of the brain functions like a command center, communicating with the rest of the body through the nervous system so that the person has the energy to fight or flee.' This means that our brain reacts on its own accord to situations and triggers a response in us, essentially to protect us.

Our early ancestors were often faced with genuine threats, such as sabre-toothed tigers. They had two immediate responses – to either stand their ground and put up a fight, or flee the scene and run to safety, hence fight or flight. This reaction evolved to protect us so we can either attack the danger in front of us or get out of harm's way.

However, in today's world, we need to update our minds to realise that most of the time, there is no immediate threat in front of us – no sabre-toothed tigers patrol the streets! Although GP'ers are incredibly unlikely to be faced with a huge man-eating animal, our bodies are still reacting to perceived 'threats' by going into fight-or-flight mode. We feel as though we need protection, despite there being no actual imminent danger or physical attack in front of us.

In times of panic, we believe that there is a risk present, and our body reacts. That's because the fight-or-flight response can also be triggered by our internal threats, such as a memory or an upcoming worry. Our panic can therefore be rooted in the past, here in the present or even focused on the future. On sensing danger, our brains automatically release a concoction of hormones, including adrenaline, to ensure that we are ready to jump into action. In these moments, our body prioritises the survival response and shuts down non-essential functions, so that we lose our clarity, perspective and confidence. Nothing rational or logical whatsoever seems to run through our heads!

Many sensations can happen in our body once the fight-or-flight response has been triggered. It is different for everyone, but here are some common symptoms:

- Our breath quickens and becomes shallow, usually in our upper chest.
- Our palms begin to sweat.
- Our tummies do somersaults.
- Our vision narrows.
- Surges of energy push us into action.
- Our blood starts pumping faster.

It is often disconcerting to have this rush of power coursing through our body; we are unable to think clearly or rationally. This head-to-toe reaction enhances our panic, as there is often no clear reason in front of us for feeling that way. If there is a reason, it can appear insignificant or unworthy; the cause does not warrant the response. What is happening inside our body can feel like unfamiliar territory, so we become confused as we try to work out what the perceived threat is. Our emotional response can also go through the roof, which can make us feel sensitive, exhausted or even completely blank.

Importance to GP'ers

It is important to know that our body can jump into fight-or-flight mode. If there is a perceived threat to us – whatever it may be – we can guarantee that we will respond in some way. This can be reacting in body and mind, to varying levels, dependent on the situation and the individual.

However, knowledge is power. By tracking our triggers and trying to read the signals, we can develop an improved, and far more helpful, response. In other words, by understanding how our body is going to react, we can deal with it faster and better.

On top of this, awareness that our body and mind is reacting to a *perceived* threat is useful. In that moment we can calm ourselves by understanding that there is not a sabre-toothed tiger in front of us. Instead, we may be faced with a deadline from a demanding boss or arriving at a party where we don't know anyone. We could be dealing with an unhappy customer or running late for an appointment. Any of these everyday occurrences can trigger the fight-or-flight response.

Jump into Action

The first time you experience this fight-or-flight response, you might feel bizarre and unsure of what is happening to you. It's all right – it will pass. Remember, you will be okay. Here are a few tips to help you manage your response.

+ *Write in a journal*

The most productive way to handle these stressful situations is to write down the emotions you are feeling and the physical reactions you are having. Imagine you are an outsider, looking at yourself from a distance, and notice how you are reacting. It is helpful to pop these reactions in columns, like I've done here.

Date	Trigger	Emotional response	Physical response	What I am proud of	What I want to remind myself of next time
8th May	Important phone call	Tearful, on edge	Felt sick, sweaty palms; slightly short of breath	Calmed instantly when using some of the techniques I've learnt – specifically breathing deep	It is not permanent; I will get through it

By being aware of your physical sensations, you can easily and quickly spot these issues in the future and thus calm yourself before your anxiety escalates. By knowing your triggers, you can take control earlier.

Also ask yourself: What is the valid reason for feeling as you do? The point of asking is to find out how rational and reasonable your anxiety is. It can also give you clarity on what is actually causing your reactions; perhaps it is something other than the 'surface' problem.

+ *Take a breath*
Bring back a sense of calm and clarity by breathing very deeply, slowly and fully. When all rational thoughts have abandoned us and our body starts to pump adrenaline faster, just breathe deeply – right into the pit of your belly (the next chapter provides in-depth guidance). If you are struggling to concentrate and slow your breathing, try closing your eyes to help you focus on your breath moving in and out of your body. This will ensure that the adrenaline will start to get under control, and your stress response will slow down. Remember as you are breathing to tell yourself, 'This is completely normal, and by breathing deeply, I know that I can calm myself down right here, right now.'

+ *Shift it*
Depending on where you are, try to expel some energy in a new environment. Go for a short walk, carry out an errand or do some form of exercise. If you are stuck in an office and cannot leave, go to the bathroom or meeting room.

In this new space, stretch up tall and then flick out your hands to your sides. As you do so, imagine that the nervous energy is flicking out of your fingertips and dripping away from you.

Next, run your hands down your arms, creating friction, to get rid of the energy through your fingertips.

Finally, jiggle your whole body – shaking the anxiety out of your system.

+ *Go with it!*

We can be scared by the power of our body when we are panicking. Rather than fight it, go with it! Try riding with the energy: match it or even attempt to raise it; shout, curl up, dance, yelp, make fists or hop around. By physically responding, it's possible that rather than resisting the energy, we actually feel a huge sense of relief in accepting it. Roll with it.

+ *Change your perspective*

Imagine you have a camera and you can decide if you wish to zoom in or zoom out on what's happening to you right now. Playing with distance gives you the chance to gain some perspective on the current situation.

Start by 'zooming in' on something very specific, such as the colour, smell and shape of an object in front of you. It can be anything; just get present and notice what you see. What stands out to you? (We'll discuss being present more in 5.1, *Meditation & Mindfulness*.)

Or, you can try 'zooming out' and gain a different view of the situation. For example, imagine you are soaring high in the air. Perhaps you are in a helicopter or you are a bird. Now, look down from that angle. What do you notice from up here? How does the problem look from this perspective?

From this viewpoint, think about this particular moment in the bigger scale of your life. How important is it? Will you remember it in a week or a month or a year? Will it last forever? How does it sit in the timeline of your life?

+ *Practise positive visualisation*

Positive visualisation can change your perspective as well. Picture your thoughts as swirling objects that finally manage to settle down. For example, imagine you are in a storm when the fight-or-flight response kicks in. With practice and in time, you can get yourself to the centre, into the eye of the storm. Here everything is quieter, calmer and clearer.

Or picture a bowl in which sand has been rushing around, creating low visibility. Finally the sand settles at the bottom of the bowl, and you can see again. Or perhaps it might be a tempestuous sea, but in a moment the sea calms and becomes still – the top of it like a sheet of glass.

Is there an image that works for you, such as a place in nature that makes you feel calm and safe? Perhaps it is recalling a happy moment when you felt peaceful and in control. Whatever it is, bring it to life now – draw and represent it, write down a vivid description; adding details such as texture, smell and sounds will help make the visualisations more impactful. If this doesn't work, try finding a song that represents it or tell someone about it. Play around with how you bring it to life and see what works best for you.

My Experience

I can remember clearly the first time I had a panic attack – I was terrified. I completely lost control of my body and could not think rationally. I felt sick, shook, sweated, had blurred vision and no coherent thoughts, and ultimately felt that the world was closing in on me. Initially I wanted to 'fight', but in the end I felt so horrific that I took 'flight'.

What I have since learnt about the fight-or-flight response has helped me cope. Just by having an awareness that my body was reacting has been a comfort, as I can separate the physical from the emotional. I have written down all my responses to panic and have tried all the ideas I've listed here. In different moments, different techniques work. Therefore, I constantly revisit these resources to make them stronger and keep them fresh in my mind so I can access them immediately and help bring my panic back under control.

I particularly enjoy the flicking exercise. Although simple (and a little silly), it really does get rid of the excess energy when

I feel 'whizzy' and reduces the feelings of panic.

Regardless of what techniques help you, the most important takeaway is reminding yourself that the anxiety will pass – everything does, and so too will the panic.

Go for It

Jot down which ideas in this chapter you want to explore further. Once you have decided on a couple of things that might work for you, get practising. Try rehearsing when you feel that you are not under threat in any way. This is important, as you can familiarise yourself with the tools when you are feeling in control and strong. Then the next time you feel your body reacting, you can implement all you have learnt. Practice makes perfect.

Whatever you decide, be safe in the knowledge that people go through the fight-or-flight response all the time. You are not alone, and you will get through it.

It will not last forever. It will pass.

1.2 Breathe Deep

Whatever you do, do it well.
– Walt Disney

Snapshot

Breathing is critical for our survival. Yet in times of panic and anxiety, it can be challenging to take deep, slow and powerful breaths. It can feel as though we are clogged up and choking on stale air, and we struggle to get fresh and rejuvenating new air into our lungs. Consequently, our breath becomes short, rapid and high up in our chest rather than deep down in our belly. To add to the panic, we may worry that we are unable to breathe and our breathing feels insufficient.

To reduce the panic, we need to focus on deep belly breathing – getting oxygen to all those dark and closed places that are yearning to get fresh, clean and cool air.

Moreover, for our mind to function well, we need to get sufficient oxygen into our brains. In all anxious situations, clarity of mind is one of the first things that seems to go out of the window, despite being the thing that we crave most at the time. By breathing properly, we can quickly calm ourselves down – both mentally and physically. Breathing is the single most important way that we can slow down our heart rate. Doing so will send a message to the rest of the body that all can resume as normal. Our brains will feel calmer, and we will be able to think clearer.

Importance to GP'ers

For Generation Panic, our breathing is the most powerful tool that we have in our toolbox. By focusing on our breath, we can distract our attention from the anxiety and concentrate on the simple act of our breath moving in and out of our body. It is a clear, easy and reassuring task when our days become chaotic and the panic rises. In breathing deeply, we can bring our body and mind together and create a sense of stillness and control. Win-win.

Jump into Action

+ *And breathe*

Try the following relaxation techniques to help you focus on your breath:

- Find a comfortable sitting position, with your feet squarely on the floor and your palms relaxed face-down in your lap. Lower yourself fully into the seat and sit up straight so that the air can travel freely down your body.
- Now relax your shoulders and jaw (by wiggling or stretching them out) and exhale.
- Next, slowly breathe in deeply for seven seconds through your nose. Hold it for seven seconds and then breathe out through your mouth for seven seconds. Remember this 7-7-7 as it will come up continuously and serves as a great reminder.
- Repeat (at least three times, but ideally more).

If it helps, then gently rest your hand on your tummy to be able to feel the breaths coming in and out properly. Become aware of the new air coming into your body and exhaling the stale and unwanted air. Take your deep breaths to the places where tension and anxiety fester, and on the exhale let that tension and anxiety go. Focus solely on your breathing – nothing else.

If thoughts arise, let them pass and float off by observing, not engaging, them. When your mind wanders, gently bring your attention back to your breath.

Try to make sure that your breaths are smooth and fluid, without any gasping.

NB: If you feel that you are not getting enough air, remember that is normal when feeling anxious or suffering from a panic attack. But do try to keep going and find a breathing pace that works for you.

+ *Go one step further*
Imagine that the pit of your stomach has lots of dark nooks and crannies – different areas that haven't felt the experience of new air in many days. They are desperate for some fresh air.

In your mind's eye, as you breathe deeply, let the new air you are inhaling reach these dark and untouched places – almost like little caves. In doing so, take positive energy and light to where it is needed, and breathe out the negative darkness. Remember you have replaced that darkness with something far more powerful and useful. Picture your stomach unfolding; the caves are being expanded, and your stomach is instead an open unrestricted plane or a wide accessible sphere. Whatever you imagine, see the air circulating freely and deeply. The flow of air is fluid, and there are no obstacles or difficult places to reach. If there are still blockages, focus on bringing new oxygen into this place. Create a rhythm with your breath, and find a pace that works for you.

+ *Make it rain*

Close your eyes and imagine that you are standing under a calm waterfall. Let the waterfall wash over your head, over your shoulders and down your back, and as it does, breathe deeply using the 7-7-7 method. As the calm water continues to cascade over your body, feel the peaceful fluidity. Let it wash your anxieties and worries off your body, downstream, and just stand in this moment. Then breathe deeply yet again. And another deep breath, letting go. If you are still feeling restless, get the waterfall to move even slower, and be specific: imagine you can feel its magic, its peaceful, calming waters wash over your forehead, your eyes and your nose.

+ *Find peace and quiet*

When panic starts to rise from deep within us, we need to remember that we can control and overcome anxiety by using our breath. Take the necessary time to get air into the places that need it. If you are in a group situation when you start to panic, excuse yourself and find a quiet spot, like a bench outside. Remember, taking a break to breathe will benefit you; it will make you calmer and able to think clearly.

NB: Practise all the recommendations I've provided even when you are feeling strong and positive. Take some deep breaths, and notice what happens in your body. Even outside of anxious moments, breathing well will benefit you hugely, both physically and emotionally.

My Experience

The most powerful tool in my box is 7-7-7. I cannot emphasise enough how much I use it. I have realised that my breathing is the easiest way to control my panic and anxiety levels. In any given moment, I often catch myself breathing short, shallow breaths – without thought, my breath is naturally high up in my chest. As soon as I do the 7-7-7 and breathe fully into the depths of my tummy, I immediately feel calmer and happier, and I gain clarity. By consciously focusing on my breath, anxiety fades. Even if I am not able to manage deep belly breaths because I am feeling too panicky, my awareness and attention has a positive impact on my anxiety level.

Likewise, I find that getting someone else to talk through the waterfall image while I breathe is relaxing and calming – it feels like a break from anxiety. No matter what breathing methods here help you best, work on improving your breath so that it becomes second nature to you.

Go for It

If you are ever feeling anxious, deep breaths should be your first port of call. Your breath is your ally. Even one deep, full-belly breath can have a profound impact. Just remember to make it a habit so it's an easy tool to call upon.

REMINDER: Your breath is *always* there.

1.3 The Heartbeat Tapper

Be not afraid of going slowly. Be afraid only of standing still.
– Chinese Proverb

Snapshot

When having a panic attack or feeling anxious, our heart rate can skyrocket. It can escalate out of control, usually unexpectedly and quickly. Those having a panic episode often say it is like having a heart attack – clearly not a feeling we want to experience.

The good news is that we can develop control of our heart rate in any moment through breathing and other techniques; we just need to consciously remember to do it and focus our mind (1.2, *Breathe Deep*).

When experiencing a panic attack, our body can react in various ways. We can think of our heart as the captain of our ship, it has the ability to direct and inform many other parts of our body. If the captain of a ship loses the plot or goes for a tea break, it is likely that the rest of the crew will follow suit. The crew will have no direction, as there is no one to set the agenda and look up to. Pandemonium and chaos can ensue.

So, the point of this is to ensure that the captain – i.e., our heart – tries to remain as calm as possible. This will allow the heart to send out the right messages to the rest of our body to help regain control.

By breathing deep and finding a comfortable position with

both feet firmly grounded, we can start to calm our heart rate. Then by gently tapping on our wrist, we can begin to guide the tempo we wish our heart rate to beat at. By focusing solely on the speed and the sensation of the tapping (which will be slower than our current heart rate), we can begin to calm ourselves in that very moment. This method of controlling our heart rate to reduce anxiety is what can be thought of as *the heartbeat tapper*.

Importance to GP'ers

Being able to control our heart rate can ensure that we lower our anxiety levels, and that if we do have a panic attack, we can calm ourselves far more quickly. Rather than having a blank mind and being unable to gather our thoughts, we can find peace by getting our senses back.

The heartbeat tapper can also act as a diversion – it gives our mind something to concentrate on that is not our escalating panic. And the attention this requires is minimal – our brain can still do this under immense pressure.

Jump into Action

+ *Spot the signs*

If you feel the onset of your indicators of anxiety or a panic attack (1.1, *Fight or Flight*), take a moment to pause and be aware. Remember, everyone is different, and these reactions can be anything from sweaty palms to blackout. Be aware of what your *own* indicators are so you know when to take action.

+ *Tap, tap, tap away*

Find a calming place where you can be alone and create some space around you. If you can't leave where you are (e.g., if you are in a meeting), don't worry, as you can still do the following. Just tailor it to what works best for you in that situation. For example, rather than 7-7-7, do 4-4-4, and do the heartbeat tapper technique under the table. Or come up with an excuse to leave the room or dinner table for a few minutes.

First, find a comfortable position and plant both of your feet firmly and squarely on the floor. Sit up straight to ensure that air can move freely down through your body.

Now take five deep breaths using the 7-7-7 technique. Then, turn over one of your hands, so your wrist is facing up and lay it gently in your lap. Rest your other hand's forefinger and middle finger on the wrist, right over where your veins run down. Now gently tap those fingers up and down in a constant, slow rhythm. Count off 'one and two and three and ...' as you tap to make sure you are trying to slow your heart rate. Challenge yourself to go as slowly as you can. Once you get to ten, start again at one.

As you do this, remember to breathe – as steadily and as calmly as you can.

Whilst you continue to tap on your wrist, say to yourself, 'I am calming the leader of the ship to ensure that he or she can update the rest of the crew that I am okay.' Or alter to whatever phrase resonates best with you.

+ *Get to the heart of it*

A modification of this technique is to put your hand on your heart instead of your lap. With your other hand, gently tap on your heart, or perhaps your knee, with the same method you just learned.

If you are struggling to slow your heart rate with the heartbeat tapper, get a friend or someone nearby to slowly count with you or tap your wrist.

My Experience

When panic rises through my body and I feel that I am losing control, I am often brought back down to reality by this easy technique. The beauty of it is its simplicity; once I got my head around the concept, I found that I could do it regardless of how anxious I was. I often do it quietly whilst waiting for things, such as going to a meeting or getting on stage, often in the bathroom or under a table to be subtle and keep myself calm. I imagine a drummer on a ship (like at the front of a dragon boat) who is beating rhythmically in time, so that the rest of my body follows suit. It works for me – the challenge is just remembering to do it.

Go for It

Bring your captain (heart) back to the helm of the ship. Let the captain lead and direct your course, however rough the seas might get.

1.4 Your Body Speaks

Our bodies change our minds, and our minds can change our behaviour, and our behaviour can change our outcomes.
– Amy Cuddy

Snapshot

Lots of research shows that the posture of our bodies can have a huge impact on our outlook and frame of mind. Simply said, our body can influence our thoughts. For example, when we are particularly anxious, we sometimes describe ourselves as feeling 'scrunched', 'doubled over', 'crushed', 'squeezed' or 'tight'. It is amazing that when someone is feeling down, you can see it in their bodies – their shoulders may be hunched, and they can even appear heavy and lacklustre. This is because our muscles tense up when we are feeling anxious, and our body reflects our emotions. Some people cross their legs, start to fidget or bite

21

their nails.

Our body really does speak, and we need to observe the non-verbal communication by listening to the messages it is trying to tell us. This will enable us to learn how we truly communicate when we're anxious and, if we want to, how we can change it.

Often, our brains are intent on saying, 'I am totally fine,' when something much deeper is stirring. Our body represents these emotions continuously. If we are trying to be strong and brave all the time, our body will eventually speak the truth and tell us what is really going on. So although we tell ourselves, 'I'm doing fine today,' our body will let us know that we are anything but fine and instead reveal our vulnerabilities.

Anxiety is one indicator of when we are doing far too much, miles outside our comfort zone, or perhaps pushing ourselves to unhealthy limits. It is ultimately a reaction from our body. The way we deal with this pressure is insightful, and by studying ourselves, we can learn to love the signals that our body tells us. We'll know to ask, 'What messages is my body trying to communicate to me?' or 'What is important about the way my body is changing depending on what is in front of me?'

Importance to GP'ers

Our body feeds our emotional state, and conversely, our mind also influences our body. They are inextricably linked and greatly impact one another. Therefore, something as simple as good posture can release the tension anxiety creates in us.

Understanding and focusing on how much the body and mind are linked will enable us to try to bypass the destructive messages running through our heads. If we physically hold our body in a positive manner, we can help our mind catch up and influence our brain in the *right* way. Or vice versa – our body is on what seems like a foreign planet, and our mind wants it to come back down to earth!

Don't forget that our brains are taking note of the non-verbal communication in our body. Our mind often holds on to the messages that our body communicates. Therefore, if we change our body language, our judgement can shift, and we can feel far happier.

Jump into Action

+ *Grin away*

It is amazing how much of an impact smiling can have on your state. Sure, you might not feel like grinning when you're feeling anxious, but it really can shift your attitude. Even a small one creates a positive feedback loop to yourself. Go on, try it now.

+ *Listen to your body speak*

Imagine that your body is trying to send you a message. Even if you do not feel anxious, notice what is occurring in your body. Where are you feeling an emotion? How are your hands reacting? What do your legs feel like? Are your shoulders hunched? Is your jaw clenched? If you were unable to communicate through speech, then what would your body be saying on your behalf? As you read this sentence, freeze your body and notice what it is telling you. If your body could talk, what would it say to you? What is the true message?

+ *Stand tall*

Now let's have a little fun! Let us try to reduce our anxiety with this quick exercise.

Stand up, with your feet shoulder-width apart – either at home or grounded on the grass outside, if that helps. Feel the energy coming up through the floor or ground. Imagine that the ground is giving you strength. Let a smile take over your face. Let it move across your lips and start radiating out.

Take two deep breaths, and then flick off the extra energy (just like in *Fight or Flight*). Start at the top of your shoulders. Place your left hand on your right shoulder and run it down your arm, flicking the extra energy off the end of your fingertips. Get that surplus whizziness off you. You can be as slow or fast, soft or hard as you like. Play around to see what works for you, and repeat as much as you need to.

Now as you stand still, take one more deep breath. Loosen out your jaw and roll your shoulders. Take another deep breath into the pit of your tummy. Now open up your chest, pulling your shoulders back and sitting up straight. Raise your eyes to at least level with your body or higher. Notice how this immediately has a positive impact on your mood. Raising your eyeline should make you feel that you have a more visual perspective, that opportunities are more open to you and things are a little clearer.

My Experience

As clichéd as it sounds, when I 'check in' with my body and ask it what is going on or how I am feeling, as long as I am open to listening to it, I receive accurate and honest feedback. My tense shoulders, tight jaw or stiff fingers give me clear messages. It's easy to trundle through life and rarely take the time to check in with our bodies – but our bodies tell us exactly what is going on and often what we need.

Moreover, sitting straighter and smiling also impacts my mood. These are small tweaks, but my anxiety recedes if I am standing proud with my shoulders back while smiling. Like me, you need to continuously remind yourself of this before interacting with others, particularly if you are feeling nervous or on the back foot in some way. By listening to and shifting your body, you will change how you go into a room and your impact on others.

Go for It

Allow yourself to stand tall. Remember that your body can send messages to your brain, so use this knowledge to your advantage to start sending the best messages you can.

1.5 Cue Cards

Do what you can, with what you've got, where you are.
– Squire Bill Widener, in *Theodore Roosevelt: An Autobiography*

Snapshot

According to sources such as the National Health Service, a panic attack often lasts only twenty minutes. We can feel anxious before and after, but the actual attack will only 'survive' for that amount of time. However, those twenty minutes can feel like a lifetime. As our panic spirals to a level where our body takes over, we start to believe that the feeling will last forever and that we will never get respite from this full-body-and-mind overload.

Carrying cue cards in our pocket or bag serves as a brilliant physical reminder of what to do in a panic attack, particularly when our rational brain seems to have run for the hills and we have nothing to ground ourselves with. The cards, which you will learn how to make in a moment, are filled with rational thoughts and tips that will benefit us during a panic attack. Even knowing that the cards were created when we were feeling stronger and in control can reassure us.

Importance to GP'ers

When anxious or in the midst of a panic attack, our minds feel foggy, heavy and completely unreasonable. Our emotional mind can fuel the panic attack even further as we start to freak out that nothing is making sense. However, it is crucial that we hold on to the knowledge that we *can* get through it, and most importantly, we will. Our cue cards will help us do just that.

Jump into Action

+ *Brainstorm away*

First, find a time when you are feeling comfortable and happy. Do not do this exercise if anxiety is lurking.

Start by writing down what happens to you in a panic attack or when you are feeling anxious. On the left side of the page, note all the symptoms, however small they might be: for example, 'My shoulders get tense,' 'I feel sick' or 'I begin to sweat.' (You can add to your list from 1.1, *Fight or Flight*, or write a new one.)

Now, on the right side of the page next to each symptom, jot down ideas of how to combat it. Any idea is a good idea; sometimes the simplest or most absurd idea is what will work best for you. List as many things as you can think of. For example, next to 'My shoulders get tense' you could write, 'Go do some exercise to ease the tension; roll my shoulders; take lessons to improve my posture; research what is actually happening in this moment; talk to a friend; get a cup of tea; take ten minutes to myself; lie flat and stretch out on the grass outside; dance around; imagine that a waterfall of relaxing water is running over my shoulders; go for a swim, get a massage, etc.' (Once you have finished reading this book, this is a great exercise to revisit to add some more tips.)

Next time you are feeling anxious, try some of the ideas you have brainstormed. Don't worry – some won't work or have any impact on you. But others might bring about a sense of calm. Build on the ones that help and get curious about the impression they leave on you. How do they make you feel? What specifically calms you down – a particular word, an action, a reassurance?

What do you like about it?

After a trial period, start homing in on what is most impactful. On top of this, find any quotes or inspirational messages that resonate. Once you have pulled together all this information in your list, you can begin to create cue cards.

+ Get creative

Start to fill out the cards however you want. Consider making the writing big and clear on different coloured cards, particularly if your panic attacks blur your vision. To this point, the cue cards should contain basic instructions – merely a few words per card – so you can digest the message easier and prevent information overload.

Here are some suggestions to write on your cards, in no particular order.

- This will pass.
- Knowledge is power!
- Thoughts ➜ Physical Reaction ➜ Behaviour ➜ Thoughts (and the cycle repeats).
- Panic is a celebrity; it demands attention!
- Stop! Drop your shoulders, breathe and close your mouth.
- Let thoughts breathe … let them be.
- You can choose to do something or let it take hold.
- Change your behaviour.
- Remember the captain of the ship.
- Use my heartbeat tapper.
- You can neutralise your emotions.
- Nothing bad is going to happen to you.
- A change will take place.
- You will calm down again.
- This attack will be gone soon.
- You will feel more confident.

- Don't run away – you can do this.
- You can handle it.
- You are not in any danger.
- You will get through this.

Has something triggered your panic this time? Write it down immediately on a cue card. You can also write down your thoughts and reactions; label them for what they are.

Play around with what you write and the format of the cards. Pop them all into a stack and bring them out when you need them to see how you react to them. As you flick through them, try to focus on each one individually; read each sentence and think about its meaning before moving to the next card.

My Experience

My cue cards are now worn down and well loved. I carry them around with me when I am feeling on edge, and they feel like a security blanket. Just knowing that I have them in my handbag gives me confidence. I have used them in many times of trouble, and I've found comfort remembering that I wrote them when feeling stronger. The words on each cue card are clear, colourful and simple; most are from the example list I gave you. This concept is all thanks to my Mum, who wrote my first set when I had no idea what was going on.

Go for It

Remember to bring the cards out when needed, so don't leave home without them.

2. Stop! Think!

Everyone is a genius. But if you judge a fish on its ability to climb a tree, it will spend its whole life believing that it is stupid.
– Unknown

2.1 Heart versus Head

2.2 Acknowledgement

2.3 Do Not Live in Fear

2.4 Get Out of Your Comfort Zone

2.5 Trust Your Gut

2.6 You Are Not Alone

2.7 Learn to Love It

2.8 Happy, Healthy You

2.1 Heart versus Head

Here is my secret. It is very simple: It is only with the heart that one can see rightly; what is essential is invisible to the eye.
– Antoine de Saint-Exupéry

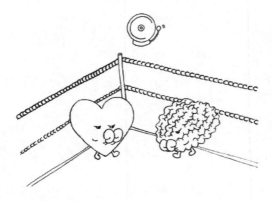

Snapshot

Normally our head rules the roost and our heart is overlooked. We rationalise thoughts in our head and tell ourselves the 'right' story of how and why we are feeling and acting as we are. By listening to our head, we do not connect to our heart and acknowledge how we really feel about something. And when we don't acknowledge how we truly feel, we bottle up our emotions and remain anxious.

For example, someone who struggles with public speaking can rationalise it in their head by telling themselves that it is merely a ten-minute speech, so it will be over soon, and also that the audience are on their side (and will most likely forget about it within a day). They can also do the trick of picturing everyone naked in the bath. Yet still, when they go on stage to present, they are overcome with nerves and lack confidence and self-belief. This person will be unable to conquer their anxiety unless they start to truly listen to their heart – and subsequently find a good balance between their heart and head.

The struggle with anxiety is often due to one of these two having the upper hand, and more often than not, the head rules. In this fast-paced and heady world, it is difficult to find a good balance between the two. Picture a bird, where one wing represents the heart and the other represents the head. When one wing dominates, the bird flies in circles. Instead, both wings need to work together to ensure that the bird can soar high and freely. We need to find the right balance of heart and head, both of which have equal value, and therefore reduce our anxiety.

Importance to GP'ers

It is important to listen to our heart. What we find there is honest and unfiltered, and it leads to new perspectives. We just need to find the time to listen to it, ask questions and get to the literal 'heart' of it.

So why do we need to listen? Because our heart can lead our mind. In other words, a reaction we feel in our heart can be a precursor to what our mind is trying to mask. If we ignore our heart, then there is disconnection between what we are feeling and what is actually happening. This is when we feel particularly anxious or our bodies react negatively, as our heart is not being listened to. In these moments, our mind panics and we cannot quite put thoughts together; everything seems overwhelming.

Our mind is creative, imaginative and free. It should be open to allow the best information to come through. By understanding the power of our mind, possibilities and new learning open up to us.

Likewise, the heart is intuitive and speaks the truth. Let's start listening more to it. At the very least, we can start listening to our heart *with* our head – hand in hand. Both parts should be given equal voice. This will ensure you are in touch with what is going on so you can manage your anxiety better.

Jump into Action

+ *Get curious!*

Notice when your head and heart speak and lead your actions. From which place do you make decisions? From where do you offer advice? How do you decide how you feel about an experience?

When faced with a difficult decision, take a few minutes (or as long as needed) to get curious as to what is occurring in your body. Is your heart being listened to? Or has your head led this decision?

+ Say it out loud!
Try to take a few seconds in any anxious moment and say, 'I need to get out of my head,' or perhaps, 'What does my heart actually think about this?' For example, when agonising over a difficult work scenario, ask yourself, 'What does my heart want?'

If you are struggling to listen to your heart, take some deep breaths (as in 1.2) and try to centre yourself. Now place one hand (or both hands if you wish) on your heart and close your eyes. Breathe into your heart. Feel the blood pulsing through it; feel the strength of the beat. Notice if it has anything to say. With practice, it will get easier to connect, and listen, to it.

My Experience

My head speaks loudly and often thinks it is 'right' by rationalising and coming up with excuses and reasons for situations when I am feeling overwhelmed. Therefore, when I feel anxious, my head tries to justify my experience, but it is often an incorrect analysis of what is actually happening. I have had to challenge myself to pause, take a deep breath and listen to my heart. Often it tells me that I am feeling far more scared or vulnerable than I care to admit. Although it first feels alarming to acknowledge these feelings, by being honest with myself, I feel reassured and once again I can breathe deeply.

Like me, you may find that your bird often uses only one wing and flies in circles! Every day, we must work on taking a more balanced approach so our lopsided bird has a smooth and balanced flight. It takes effort and conscious thought to listen to our heart, but you'll find that if you provide the safe space for it to talk, your heart has a lot to say!

Go for It

When either your heart or head doesn't have a voice, your body is aware of it and will react. Some part of you will feel out of control and not listened to. Remember that you will make better decisions when you listen to your heart *and* head and strike a balance between the two. Start flying using both wings.

2.2 Acknowledgement

It is truth that liberates, not will and effort.
– Jiddu Krishnamurti

Snapshot

Many GP'ers are determined to come across as strong, in control and excelling in life. We believe that we must always appear confident, self-assured and successful.

Therefore, when GP'ers are faced with pressure, much of the panic comes from the fear of having to admit that things aren't progressing as we had hoped – or as others wanted, since we rarely define our own version of success. Instead, it is usually imbedded in us from someone else – parents, friends, teachers, idols, etc.

For Generation Panic, acknowledging that we have a weakness – even a perceived one – is tough. In fact, it's often a foreign concept. High achievers are so determined to be awesome all the time that it can feel as though we are admitting defeat by acknowledging that we have anxiety. We have, in our eyes, failed.

Moreover, for the high-achieving Generation Panic, anxiety is an unfamiliar experience – new and unsettling. Perhaps we have excelled at school, thrived in social situations or had a booming start to our careers and have been on a steep upward trajectory. Anxiety hasn't really played a part in our lives to date.

Now, the pressure of achieving can make us feel like we're the tower in a Jenga game. We can see other people playing the game, stacking pieces on to us, making us taller, bigger and better. However, we are aware of all the cracks and gaps, and how fragile the construction is. All it would take is for one person to pull just the right piece from under us and our Jenga tower would tumble down. Smack! It would then lie in ruins on the floor and take a long time to build back up. Why get to that point? We must deal with the Jenga tower now and start taking back pieces, filling in the gaps and playing our own game. We can do this by acknowledging that we suffer from anxiety, and that, at times, we need help.

Importance to GP'ers

Anxiety is fast becoming a top concern for millions of people. The National Alliance on Mental Illness (NAMI) states that 'anxiety disorders are the most common mental health concern in the United States. An estimated 40 million adults in the U.S. (18%) have an anxiety disorder.' And for the UK, the *Journal of Psychopharmacology* reported in 2013 that there were 8.2 million cases of anxiety. Comparable, remarkable figures exist worldwide.

Acknowledging that you fall into this camp, particularly when you have been deemed a strong person throughout your life, is difficult. It can feel like defeat. But it is the truth, and you are not alone.

Only through acknowledgement will we be truly released and start to feel freer and lighter. It is like a pressure cooker. The more we uphold this fake version of ourselves that is 'totally fine', the more pressure builds to live up to the image we have created. We need to release some of the steam, or the pressure cooker will blow.

We also need to remember that we are human beings. As humans, we will make mistakes. It can be frustrating, but there is no need to punish ourselves. Instead, be kinder to yourself; acknowledge that you've made a mistake, learn from it and then move on. No one is perfect, and there is no exception to the rule.

Jump into Action

+ *Mega mind mapping*

Make a 'mind map', which is essentially brainstorming different ideas on one page and linking them with lines so that you can see the connections and the full picture. Write down everything that is worrying you right now. Look at all the concerns and see which ones create an emotional or a physical reaction. Now step back from them and just notice what you notice. For example, your 'mind map' might include going to an event this week, or the upcoming meeting with your manager. Do they make you feel sick or nervous, or does your emotional side react by telling you, 'You are not good enough to do this'? Just acknowledge, without judgement, what you feel here.

+ *Define your version of success*
- Brainstorm what success truly means to you. Not anyone else's version, but yours. What are the components? What would it look like? Or feel like?
- If you could fast-forward five years and see your most successful life, what would you see? What would be happening? Who would you be? What would you be most proud of? Jot it all down.

+ *Honesty is the best policy*

Be honest with how you are feeling. Trying to mask it to prove to everyone that you can cope and have everything under control is like sweeping dust under the carpet; the bulge will build over time only to trip you up later. Allow yourself to express what is going on to those you trust – they are there to support you. There is nothing wrong or abnormal with you for having the feelings you are having, even fear or anger. Say what you think – no matter how crazy or irrational it might sound. Blurt it out now, and be honest.

For more about confiding in those close to you, read 2.6, *You Are Not Alone*, and 3.5, *Build a Support Network*.

+ *Say it out loud*

The most important thing here is to simply acknowledge your anxiety out loud. Stand in front of a mirror and say out loud, clearly and calmly:

- 'I have anxiety.'
- 'I am not perfect.'
- 'I acknowledge that I am human and make mistakes.'

Add to this list or change the wording as you feel necessary. Likewise, play around with the delivery and stance – does the message change if you hold your shoulders back and speak in a low, gravelly voice versus a higher-pitched voice with your shoulders hunched? Determine whether a particular tone or body stance gets the best reaction out of you.

Likewise, notice if something jars you, such as the word *perfect*. Ask what that bodily reaction or resistance is trying to tell you (1.4, *Your Body Speaks*).

+ *Jenga*

Buy a Jenga game and write on each piece thoughts that come

to mind. You could write down all the expectations that others have put on you, or everything that is worrying you. You might choose to write who you want to be and how you want to conduct yourself, or perhaps what you want to acknowledge about your anxiety. So, if you chose the last example, you could write on one piece 'Honest' and another one 'I have anxiety.' Build the tower and play the game. In doing so, you can reduce your anxiety.

My Experience

Acknowledging my anxiety has been a huge hurdle for me, as much of my identity is wrapped up in being strong and confident. Some people were surprised when I admitted to having panic attacks and anxiety, as I appeared to have everything under control. I felt weak and embarrassed when I started telling people about what I had been going through, and it took me a long time to pluck up the courage to talk about it openly. When I did, though, I was bowled over by the support I received and the relief from having been open and honest.

For me one of the most powerful action points here is standing in front of the mirror and admitting it out loud. It seems silly and I felt self-conscious, but you'd be surprised how powerful it is. I have also enjoyed writing my own Jenga game, as I love games and the metaphor speaks to me.

Go for It

It is normal to resist acknowledging your anxiety, but only in doing so can you be free. Acknowledgement goes a long way towards accepting, and therefore reducing, your anxiety.

2.3 Do Not Live in Fear

The only thing we have to fear is fear itself.
– Franklin D. Roosevelt

Snapshot

One of the biggest drawbacks of suffering from panic attacks is living in fear of the next one. We are in a constant state of nervousness, and our body feels as though it is continuously on high alert as we wait for the next bout of anxiety to hit. The dread of the next attack will, in itself, fill us with anxiety. It is distressing and exhausting to live this way. This fear stops us from truly living the lives we want to, as we are terrified that we will be unable to handle whatever is coming.

It is as though every morning, we get ready for battle. When we wake up, we put on heavy chain mail, a clunky helmet and war paint on our faces. It is mentally exhausting to do this every day just to tackle the world – let alone how awkward and heavy it is to carry around with us. Being constantly ready for the war with anxiety is downright draining.

Yet, we are forever worried of another attack, and it can hound us more than the attack itself. Ironically, if we think it will happen, the likelihood is that it will happen. Emerson once said, '[You are] what [you] think about all day long.' If we are thinking about fear, there's one guess how we will end up! It is self-destructive to be consumed with the *thought* of a panic attack occurring.

Fear can be described as the paparazzi – it is always chasing us down, whichever way we try to escape it. Like the paparazzi, the dread of having a panic attack feasts off low moments. As a result, we become terrified of being caught out or trapped, and the apprehension of attending a meeting, a dinner or another event can be overwhelming. It spirals from here: our self-confidence diminishes, and particular situations can hold extraordinary weight; we do anything to avoid them.

However, the fear is, more often than not, far worse than the reality.

Importance to GP'ers

To some extent we all need anxiety and fear in our lives – it helps us to survive and feel truly alive. It is a great reminder that we are human and living in this very moment. We just need to ensure that the obstructing and damaging parts of fear are under control, and remind ourselves that we can handle them just fine. Realising that this is the case is a vital part of the coping process. Stop avoiding! Stop dodging! It will ease the tension.

We should not live in fear of having another panic attack. The best way to combat fear is with action to move forward. Procrastination and delay just feed it, making the beast bigger and stronger. We cannot let the *fear* of a panic attack win. Instead, let's move forward and conquer it by taking that initial step into action.

Be aware that the *fear* of having a panic attack or feeling anxious is just that – fear. This is compared to the relatively small chance that a panic attack becomes a reality. They say that 90 per cent of what we worry about never happens. That means only 10 per cent of our fears become a reality. So our worries have little chance of coming to fruition. The irony is that the amount of time spent having a panic attack is small compared to the 'worry time' that we allow ourselves to feel.

Let's also begin to hold ourselves kindly. Fear will continue to be present as we move forward and grow, expanding out of our comfort zone (see 2.4). When we push our boundaries, we guarantee that fear will show up in the face of uncertainty. Yet we just need to get on and do it, continually reminding ourselves that we are not alone and it is okay to feel this anxious; we do not need to fear the fear.

Finally, we need to trust ourselves and know that we will handle whatever comes our way. We will have already overcome hurdles, and this knowledge of past experiences where we have triumphed will help us combat fear. Start believing that you are capable and have great resources to get through anything (particularly once you've finished reading this book). Fear is squashed by action, and our ability to get through difficult moments is a wonderful reminder that we can, and will, overcome.

Jump into Action

+ *Reality check*

Consider which events fuel your anxiety. Odds are that you have either overestimated the potential for a meltdown or you have underestimated your ability to get through it. By writing it down on paper, you can gather your thoughts, as well as identify any related triggers, such as a noise or an image. This will help you to understand your panic more.

Work out the emotions that are linked to the worry. For example, are you scared that you will be caught out? Scared that you will have a bodily response you cannot control? Afraid of other people's reactions? Use the following table to help you brainstorm:

Event	Time	Reaction	Fear/Other Thoughts?
Internal meeting	10 a.m.	On edge, a little distracted, restless	Bright lights of meeting room – nowhere to hide.
Dinner with friends	7 p.m.	Anxious – very sweaty and jumpy	Late night, end of the day, tired. Worried about other people's reactions to me. Will have nothing to say.

Now brainstorm a few coping mechanisms that can help you combat the fears in these situations. What action can you take? Often any kind of action is better than nothing. For example, if you fear you will not be able to escape a situation in which panic has overridden your rational brain, think of a sentence that can ensure you can leave if you want to – even something as simple as, 'Apologies, I am not feeling very well; I am just going to pop out.'

Then you can add a further two columns to your table:

Ideas of Coping Mechanisms	What Happened/The Reality
Use heartbeat tapper; calm myself in advance with deep breaths and using my body. Acknowledge how I am feeling.	Went well. Felt a little bubble of anxiety rise up, but I could manage it and move forward.
Read my cue cards beforehand and take deep breaths. Keep myself busy in the lead-up, go to the dinner, call a friend on the way – and just do it!	Sat next to a nice friend and ended up having a good time.

Play around with these coping mechanisms – there is no right or wrong answer. Likewise, don't try to overcomplicate things; often the best route forward is simple and clear.

Then there's trial and error. Put things into practice and see whether they work. Even if they do not influence you in a positive way, do not worry as it is all part of the learning process. Get curious about your reactions to events and learn from them. Now review, change, learn, repeat, review, change, learn, and repeat – you get the picture. Through the ups and downs, there's masses we can learn. Absorb the learning and let it propel you even further for the next time.

Add two final columns to your chart for what you have learnt/ what surprised you and also what are you proud of:

What I've Learnt/What Surprised Me	What I'm Proud Of
I was able to manage the anxiety bubble.	I stayed in the meeting until the end.
I was able to enjoy myself – forgot about my anxiety.	I went in the first place.

Chances are this will work to help you reduce your fear around having a panic attack. If it does not leave an impression on you, then do not worry; this task just might not be for you.

+ Saboteurs

Another way to lessen the fear is to label the part of you that is worrying and living in dread; we call this voice and/or feeling our Saboteurs. Therefore, you can directly respond to this part of you and create a dialogue (similar to the exercise in 4.2, *Saboteurs*). Let's say that you call this voice 'Fearful Fred'. Every time Fearful Fred raises his ugly head and makes you feel on the back foot, you can say, 'Oh, hello, Fearful Fred, nice of you to come by, but you are really not needed at this particular moment. Why don't you go and make yourself useful elsewhere? Busy yourself with organising my desk today rather than bothering me – thank you.'

All the while, remember to breathe deep using 7-7-7, and repeat.

+ *Spot the difference*

Let's distinguish between excitement and anxiety, as they often get mixed up. For example, if your heart rate rises because you have run somewhere, are looking forward to meeting someone, or feel excitement and good anticipation in advance of something like a party, your mind can begin to immediately process your increased heart rate as a threat or think something has turned for the worse.

Write down five to ten ways that make you feel excited or energetic. Now compare how that feels in your body to when you are anxious.

Use this knowledge (and the differentiators) to check in and be more conscious of what is physically happening in your body. Do not scan through your body looking for emotions that might indicate anxiety. Waking up each morning and self-prophesising with 'Oh, I feel this, so I am going to be anxious today' does not help. It is about merely noticing and instead saying something along the lines of, 'Hi there, anxiety; with you I'm going to have a great start to the day.' Begin the day on the front foot, as you will be more likely to set off in a positive direction.

+ *Daydreaming*

Imagine that your anxiety left you this morning and you woke up feeling great. What would you do differently? What would happen? What would you be proud of by the end of the day? Knowing these answers can inspire you to do something new, challenging or empowering; take back control and ensure that anxiety is on the back burner.

My Experience

I still struggle with this concept of living in fear, as I often feel fear before some situations – particularly important meetings, when I need to speak publicly, and large parties. I worry that I will feel anxious and on the back foot. This can make the initial moments of those situations even more tense, as I begin to feel queasy, my palms start to sweat and my blood pumps harder. I practise the techniques mentioned here, particularly noticing what is happening, to make me feel stronger. I find that I get most out of the chapter's techniques when I am talking to my coach, as I raise my own awareness by talking about it, and I have someone to encourage me and act as a sounding board. You might be different, and this chapter may speak to you – at the very least, like me, just having an awareness is beneficial.

Go for It
Don't fear the fear! Instead, bypass it by jumping into action.

2.4 Get Out of Your Comfort Zone

A ship is safe in harbour, but that is not what ships are built for.
– John A. Shedd

Snapshot
A comfort zone is a space where you feel safe, protected and calm, a place of lower stress, lower pressure and lower risk. We often long to stay in our comfort zone, as it is a place of safety. However, it is also a place where we stay small, with no challenge and not much moving at all, let alone moving forward.

When anxiety courses through our body and we are gripped by fear, the last thing we want to do is challenge ourselves. Even the simplest tasks can become mega: for example, going outdoors, getting on public transport or going for a drink with friends. We can often relapse into a mindset that it is much safer and easier to avoid these things, and thus our comfort zone solidifies further.

To GP'ers, anything outside the comfort zone can seem like a huge risk. For example, seeing a good friend can spiral into a panic-filled situation for many reasons – how we get there, whether we'll be on time, what to order when we are with them, who is paying, whether they are going to ask us difficult questions, having nothing to say, being afraid a panic attack will occur, looking like an idiot, what they will think of us ... and on it goes. Of course, these voices are there to protect us – they want us to avoid danger by making us remain in our comfort zone. However, by playing it safe, we can actually move backwards and stop doing things that we used to do with ease.

There is a delicate balance between honouring your comfort zone and challenging yourself to move forward. At times, it is good to stretch ourselves; it can be more terrifying if we *don't* do anything and remain stuck in the small space we have created for ourselves. On the flip side, if we push ourselves too far, then anxiety can be overbearing and feel like defeat. So it's finding the right balance of stretching a little bit, swallowing the fear, and moving forward.

Knowing this, we cannot be critical of our comfort zone. This safe place lets anxiety leave us alone for a bit. We need to take a break at times from all the symptoms of anxiety.

Importance to GP'ers

It is important to push the boundaries of our comfort zone to see what we are capable of. Otherwise, we can become increasingly reclusive until all activities are too overwhelming. Look to expand your comfort zone's inner circle – even a tiny step like saying yes to an invitation. By exposing ourselves to more experiences, we will build emotional resilience and coping mechanisms to face uncertain moments. It is all about small baby steps and being realistic at the initial stages. So, plan small things to start with to achieve success. Be brave!

Often when we are feeling uncertain, scared or on the back foot, that is when real change can happen and more opportunities open up to us. Expanding our horizons and thus our comfort zone can be infinitely rewarding. Just have the courage to push the boundaries – even if only by a fraction!

Jump into Action

+ *In the zone*

What does your comfort zone look like – is it a place, a song, a feeling, a situation? What lives in the comfort zone? What happens in the comfort zone? What colour is it? What does the air taste of here? What does it feel like? What can you see? Who are you here? Draw it and bring it to life.

+ *Out of the zone*

Brainstorm what lies outside the boundaries of your comfort zone. What activities seem like a stretch for you? Don't get judgemental or question it, just notice what is beyond your limits. Metaphorically, what can you see from the centre of your comfort zone as you look out to each activity? Is it rocky or smooth? Stormy or calm? Get curious and let your imagination go. If it helps, shut your eyes to picture it. Then, jot down your reactions. How does your body feel in relation to these situations? What emotions accompany them? Again, just become aware of the feeling associated with each scenario; do not judge them. Once again, draw what you notice or write down a description.

+ *Ready, set, go!*

Now pick one simple task that will move you out of your comfort zone. Make sure that it is a manageable level of anxiety, i.e., you are not pushing yourself so far that you are worried about having a panic attack. For example, sitting in the park, walking to the shops, or making a meal.

Now give yourself a pep talk. Be positive and tell yourself something like, 'I know I can do this. I am nervous about pushing myself, but I am sure that I will learn lots and come out the other side.'

Once you have done the task, notice how you feel. What are you proud of? What would you do differently next time? What task do you want to do next?

+ *Change it up*

Make a small change to your life – perhaps trying a new restaurant, taking a different route to work or starting a new hobby. It will help expand the size of your comfort zone. By pushing yourself into new areas, you can grow and build your confidence. Get creative, and remember to start small.

If you are struggling to come up with something, change your outfit. Wear something that shows you are ready to take control and you are becoming the person you really want to be. Dressing well and being proud of your appearance can help you build your confidence and give you the 'I am ready to push my comfort zone' mentality.

And then have a go. Fear will creep in if you let your decision simmer and tell yourself, 'I will do it tomorrow,' so do it now!

On completion, return to your comfort zone and relax, re-energise and look after yourself. In this space, write down what you have learnt and how you want to challenge your boundaries again the next time.

+ *Jot it down*

It can be a pretty big deal when you venture outside your comfort zone. If you haven't done so already, journal your thoughts about how you feel, what you have taken away and what you would like to do differently next time. Most importantly, though, give yourself a pat on the back – it is not easy to take this step. It requires a lot of courage, however small you might deem the activity, so celebrate this moment. Write down what specifically you would like to celebrate, and then reward yourself with anything from a cup of tea to a special dinner.

And when you look back on the times that you have 'failed' (because there will be times when it doesn't seem to go to plan), do so positively and see what you could have learned. You cannot change what has happened, but you can alter your attitude towards it. So however 'wrong' it went, try to look for the positives. A starter for ten is that you had a go … hurrah!

+ *Onwards and upwards*
Plan for the next time you will push the boundaries of your comfort zone. Share your successes and your struggles with someone close to you. By telling a friend about it, they can help hold you accountable.

My Experience

I am very visual, so I can completely picture my comfort zone. I see a nice, big armchair for me to curl up into and step away from the world. It feels super cosy, warm and safe. When I am feeling anxious, I could stay here all day – it is just so easy to sink into the chair and shy away from everything and everyone.

On the other hand, outside of my comfort zone looks rocky, sharp and a lot greyer (along the lines of Mordor from *The Lord of the Rings*), so not hugely appealing. But I need to remember to push myself or I won't ever leave my safe armchair. I have to challenge myself to push my boundaries and try new things. They have not been that big in the past, like leaving the house. As silly as it sounds, it can sometimes feel like a huge win just getting dressed and leaving.

I also always try to celebrate and acknowledge that I have tried (even if something hasn't gone to plan). Interestingly, when

I venture into 'Mordor', it is rarely as scary as it seems. I learn lots and often feel proud of myself. As time goes on, you too will realise the power of pushing yourself and can celebrate it.

Go for It

The panic of not doing things perfectly can block us from overcoming anxiety and growing, but be safe knowing your 'messiness' is normal and is progress forward. By expanding your comfort zone, you can expand yourself. Remember you can, and you will, handle whatever comes your way.

2.5 Trust Your Gut

Life shrinks or expands in proportion to one's courage.
– Anais Nin

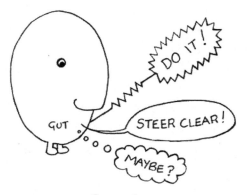

Snapshot

Our gut feeling is instinctual and instant. It holds many messages as our body reacts to experiences around us. If we learn to listen to, and honour, our gut feeling, we can feel more confident and calmer; decisions will resonate well in our body.

On the other hand, when we feel dissonant and don't listen to our gut, it is as though an internal war is waging and we are conflicted. We are disconnected to our gut when anxious, and at these times, we are acutely aware of how our body feels foreign and uncomfortable.

By understanding, connecting to and acting on our gut feeling, we can reduce our anxiety.

Remember from chapter 1.4, *Your Body Speaks*, that our physiology changes in relation to our internal struggles. It is important to understand the individual signals of when we feel dissonant or resonant. For example, home is often a calming space where we can be ourselves; everything seems to slot into place, everything is calm and there is no threat. On the flip side, the office might be the opposite, and our gut does backflips merely thinking about it, let alone being there. The internal struggle starts, and we respond to the potential danger lurking by reacting with the fight-or-flight response (chapter 1.1).

Importance to GP'ers

As GP'ers, we need to connect with our gut feeling. It communicates important messages that we can learn from, even down to triggers of how specific experiences and environments impact our anxiety. It is useful to know what makes us feel on the back foot and, by comparison, where we feel most calm and at peace. With this knowledge, we can begin to create positive anchors so that when things become more hectic and stressful, we can hold on to the previous feeling of calm – right down into our gut. For example, if we feel the anxiety starting to rise up through our body on the Tube on our way to work, we can go back and revisit the sensation, feeling and memory of a different place, and instead anchor ourselves in a more positive and calm moment. This allows the previous resonant experience to give us strength and confidence in our gut.

Jump into Action

+ *Find & connect*

Take a moment to ask yourself a few questions: Where does your gut feeling manifest in your body? What does it look like? What noise does it make? What sensations are you aware of right now? What decisions can you make here? Do you listen to your gut feeling? Do you respond to it and take action? What is one thing you could do to connect more easily to your gut feeling? Have any of your answers surprised you in any way?

+ Big-up resonance

Write down or express in some way (draw, dance, sing, anything!) what happens when you are feeling resonant. What does it actually *feel* like? Can you taste, smell or hear anything in particular? Set a goal to get to this state of resonance when dissonance settles in. For example, you might picture a smooth, flowing river or imagine being in your kitchen at home – wherever you feel at your calmest. If it is somewhere that is physically easy to access (for example, being in the park), every time you go there, enhance the feelings and be present – consciously take everything in to help make the anchor more vivid.

+ Keep a daily journal

Keep a journal of your day and observe when you feel dissonant and when you feel resonant. Perhaps write the dissonant and resonant situations in different colours or columns to make them clear. Ask yourself if there are any specifics worth noting, such as, 'I felt calm and relaxed overall but occasional fluttering and a little sweaty when I think of the upcoming presentation at the office on Wednesday.' The more detail, the better, as knowledge is power. Add to it what was happening in your gut and, most importantly, whether you listened to your gut feeling.

Go back and look at your journal after a few days with the benefit of hindsight. As you now have the ability to step back from it, ask yourself: Do you notice anything? Are there any themes? Do you want to do anything about your response for the next time?

+ *Decide you're (not) going in circles*

If you start to feel on edge, remind yourself of where you want to get to, your place of resonance. Think about what it feels like when your gut feeling works in your favour (for example, when you're picturing yourself relaxing in your favourite chair in your sitting room with the sun on your face). When the anxiety starts to rise, in your mind's eye, draw two circles on the floor – one where you are standing that can be labelled 'now' and the other labelled whatever your most resonant state is (for example, 'home', 'shower', 'running', 'café'). Then, step from 'now' to 'shower' (or whatever the second labelled circle is). Immediately feel how much lighter, springier and happier this place feels. This exercise is a quick and powerful way of shifting your energy.

My Experience

Our gut feeling is very strong and normally knows the best direction to take. I have no difficulty in connecting to mine and listening to it. When I do, it feels powerful and authentic; it is clear when something feels right or wrong. Although my gut might feel uneasy pushing my comfort zone, my gut, my heart of hearts, knows that it is the right thing to do.

I particularly love the circles exercise. By stepping into a different, happier circle, I feel calmer and more confident instantly. I usually picture a calming, flowing river, where I can listen to my gut with more ease and take a deep breath.

Go for It

If you struggle to feel resonance in its entirety, please don't panic. Pick the times that you feel the least anxious, when your gut feeling is calmer and you trust yourself more, and focus on that. Revisit this chapter every couple of weeks to build your strength. It will ease over time, and any win, however small, should be celebrated. From there, continue to build on the wins until you can connect, listen and act on your gut feeling with ease every day.

2.6 You Are Not Alone

We learn little from victory, much from defeat.
– Japanese Proverb

Snapshot

It is hard when going through tough times not to feel incredibly lonely. It seems as though we are the only ones who are facing challenges and totally alienated from the world around us. We ask ourselves, 'Why can't I keep up with everyone else?' or, 'Why am I struggling and everyone else seems okay?'. It is a negative questioning voice that asks us on repeat, 'Why am I not good enough?'. The questions go around and around in our head, almost as though we have a 400-metre running track in it and the interrogation keeps running on a loop. There is no stopping these questions and opinions; they are never-ending.

Stop the thoughts! If we look off the running track, spectators are cheering us on, and there might even be other runners right beside us. In short, we are not alone.

Everyone experiences anxiety in some format. Some people manage it better than others and *seem* to have things under control, but remember, appearances can be deceptive. If we dig past the surface and listen, something is increasing everyone's level of anxiety and worrying them. Even billionaires and famous people feel anxious about something, from a phobia to a stressful meeting or a pressured moment. We all go through challenging situations (it's called life!); it is how we deal with these moments as they arise that determines the outcome.

Importance to GP'ers

Anxiety is not a taboo subject, as we are not the only ones struggling (remember from 2.2, *Acknowledgement*, that millions of people deal with anxiety). We should be able to openly discuss it with those around us. Do speak up and share anxieties; only by getting support do we realise that others suffer too, and that they see in us what we see in ourselves. Therefore, if we are embarrassed or ashamed of our anxiety and keep it quiet, then others will not open up in return.

Even if we feel judged by those around us for opening up, we can be confident that they feel pressure about something. It is irrelevant when, why, how or what they feel pressure about; at some point they have felt or will feel it, even if they are not showing it now.

As GP'ers, we must also remind ourselves that what we deem to be our weakness can actually be our strength. We can use knowledge to empower ourselves and build an unshakeable level of self-belief. Also, let us appreciate that anxiety allows us to have honest discussions, which will have an impact on our relationships – they will be deeper and more honest, and most importantly, they will remind us that we are not abandoned.

Jump into Action

+ *Realise you've got company*
First, remember that the isolated, lonely place you are in is not an anomaly. Tell yourself the words: 'I am not alone – this is *not* an abnormal feeling for me to be having,' and repeat as many

times as you deem necessary. You can also remind yourself that this feeling you have right now will pass.

+ *Stay on track*

If the metaphor of the running track works for you, bring it alive. Picture yourself or your thoughts running around the track. Breathe deep and pause for a moment to notice what is around you. If you can't slow down, say 'Stop!' in a loud, clear and firm voice, speaking directly to the questions or thoughts running around the track. Then get curious about their reaction.

Now imagine that the track is on a TV screen that you can watch from a distance. You have a remote that allows you to change some variables. If the image in your mind is very slow, press 'fast forward'; if it is the opposite, then pop on the 'slow motion' button. If there are loud voices, soften them or even try putting the sound on mute. Play it in black and white or sepia and see if this changes anything. Now zoom in and out, and jot down whether this makes it better or worse. These small tweaks can have a profound impact on how you view a situation.

+ *Be brave*

Finally, get out there and talk to people. Sometimes you just need to put on your 'confident hat' (5.2) and talk to others. Ask people you admire how they deal with pressure. You will be surprised at the response you get. If you're not confident enough, try other tactics: find interesting books to read, check out forums or confide in good friends. What is one thing you could do today as a step in the right direction (e.g., sign up for an event or arrange to chat with a friend)?

My Experience

I frequently have to say 'Stop!' to the thoughts running around in my head, as they can become overwhelming. When I first began to feel anxious, I didn't know what was happening to me.

When I figured it out, I felt embarrassed that I had a 'weakness'; at the time, I felt enormous pressure to uphold a façade of confidence. When I finally realised I couldn't carry on that way, I was surprised at how many people were there for me; there were lots of people cheering me on from the side of the running track. I now talk openly about it and am always astounded at how many people go through something similar but haven't opened up. I used to feel lonely and as though I was the only one going through it all, but I have realised by opening up and being vulnerable that I truly am not alone.

Go for It

The difficulty in Generation Panic'ers opening up is that we are determined not to show any weakness; instead, we feel we must come across as strong and confident all the time. However, this mindset often feels removed from reality. You are never going to know if you are alone unless you open up and be honest. The proof is in the pudding – you will feel far more supported the more you recognise that others are going through the same thing. Get talking.

2.7 Learn to Love It

Your struggles develop your strength.
– Arnold Schwarzenegger

Snapshot

Anxiety is crippling. It chips away at our confidence and the fundamentals of who we are. Our foundations are at best rocked and at worst entirely crumbled. Fear can dominate our days, becoming our sole focus and fuelling our anxiety (2.3, *Do Not Live in Fear*).

Yet we have a choice about how to deal with it and can begin to determine our relationship with anxiety on our own terms. Our relationship with anxiety will alter how we feel every day, so let us start by realising that we can impact our thoughts and emotions (this links to 1.4, *Your Body Speaks*). We can create our own misery and we can also create our own happiness ... by choice. We have the opportunity to shape our lives by deciding how we *want* to feel.

Things happen in everyday life – that is life – but it is our *response* that will change what happens next. Time to get back into the driving seat; otherwise, this weak and scared part of us will continue to run our lives and take over complete control.

At this moment, we have a chance to decide between option A, letting anxiety define us and rule our life, and option B, learn from it and begin to love it. I know, it's ridiculous to start to love it ... however, our thinking and the way that we understand our anxiety can greatly influence the way we approach it. If we believe we can learn to love it (and subsequently, have a great relationship to it one day), then we will. But we have to believe it – and most importantly, we have to *want* to believe it. It is possible, as we are the product of our thoughts.

Take this moment, right here, right now, and decide that you want to take back the power and not let fear rule.

Importance to GP'ers

GP'ers need to decide to see every so-called defeat as an opportunity, a chance to learn and make life better. By being self-reflective, we can build ourselves up to be stronger and more resilient. Once we've done that, we can learn to love our anxiety.

In days, weeks, months and perhaps years to come, we will look back at this time of anxiety and be quite proud of ourselves. And rightly so. This time, right now, might be the most rewarding and give us the greatest insight into ourselves. We just need to have an awareness about what is occurring within us. In doing so, we have the chance to discover what motivates us and learn from our experiences.

Anxiety can offer you:

- Greater understanding of others
- Sympathy when other people are struggling in life
- The chance to be more honest with yourself
- Authenticity in your interactions with those around you
- Forgiveness towards yourself
- The realisation that you cannot control everything
- Knowledge that the drive to be perfect all the time is unsustainable

There is so much to learn, so let's start at the beginning.

Jump into Action

+ *Remember knowledge is power*

Think about when you feel anxious. Do not beat yourself up in these situations, but instead get curious. Ask yourself:

- What can you learn here?
- In your last bout of anxiety, what did you learn?
- What could you do differently next time?
- More specifically, what is one thing you could change about the way you led into it, dealt with it in the moment, or handled it in the aftermath?

- How can you implement that one variation to allow you to transform a very small part of your anxiety?
- What can you love about this experience?

Now learn, learn, and learn. Jot down what you have observed. Give yourself constructive feedback that you can take on board. Make it simple. Make it clear. Make it effective.

+ Learn to love it

In all those anxious moments, tell yourself, 'This is making me stronger. This is allowing me to be greater in all aspects of my life.' Try to remember all the positives rather than dwelling on all that is going wrong. Ask, 'How can I change negative experiences into positive ones?' List your negatives on one side and then your answers for turning them into positives on the other. For example:

Negatives	Positives
I am so anxious and on the back foot.	I am learning about my boundaries and who I have the best time with.
I feel sick and can't even move.	My body is telling me to slow down, so I won't try to fight it and will see what happens ... and breathe.

Keep practising. This is hard, but the more you reinforce positive words, images and stimuli, slowly but surely you will progress forward. Keep going and repeat the exercise as needed to make it a new and positive habit.

+ Repeat your mighty mantra

Have a daily mantra that you can use to kickstart your day. It can be anything from 'Today is going to be awesome,' to 'I am worthy of being heard' or 'I am learning from my anxiety and going to start to love it' to 'Bring it on.' Find whatever works for you and jot it down on a sticky note. Now put this reminder on the mirror where you brush your teeth so you cannot miss it.

My Experience

I have genuinely learnt to love my anxiety, at least most of the time. When I was having constant and full-blown panic attacks, I didn't think I could ever feel okay again. It was a very dark place, and I couldn't see a way out. It was the most challenging time of my life so far, without a doubt.

I have now started to love my darkest times because they taught me so much about myself and my boundaries, limits and weaknesses. This knowledge has empowered me, as I know myself far better and am more honest with myself.

And I love a mantra! I often have sticky notes all over the shower and mirror where I get ready in the morning. I change them regularly and find them very useful.

Go for It

We constantly face challenging times, as our world continues to change around us – after all, change is the one constant we can guarantee. However, our reactions to those challenges can differ hugely. If you are struggling with anxiety, give yourself an easier ride by learning to embrace it. Don't bother beating yourself up, as it is unhelpful and doesn't get you anywhere. Instead, learn to love it!

2.8 Happy, Healthy You

Every exit is an entry somewhere else.
– Tom Stoppard

Snapshot

Ridding yourself of anxiety is a 360-degree job, and we can start by looking holistically at the life that we lead. A few changes can have a profound impact on our stress levels and are worth trying, namely drinking lots of water, exercising regularly, maintaining a healthy diet, getting deep sleep, quitting caffeine and being drug-free. This topic could be a book in itself, yet here are the key headlines. All of them lead to us being happier and healthier.

Importance to GP'ers

Water

When anxious, our body works harder than normal to regulate our temperature and our reactions. In a 2018 article, 'The Effects of Anxiety on the Body', Medical News Today talks about how anxious 'people often experience hot flashes as a result of vasoconstriction. In response, the body sweats to cool down. This can sometimes be too effective and make a person feel cold.' To add to this, water is essential for daily life, but we often forget how important it is, especially for preventing anxious feelings. Our brains need water to function properly, so by drinking more, we can potentially decrease our levels of unease.

Exercise

When we are stressed, our body takes a hit. We experience a

whole range of consequences, from being sluggish and lazy on one end of the spectrum to feeling jittery, nervy and frazzled on the other end of the spectrum. When we are under pressure, exercise is an excellent way to relieve tension and get rid of extra stress. It produces endorphins that make us happy and allow us to think more clearly. Exercise also circulates our blood better, getting oxygen to all parts of our body.

The Anxiety and Depression Association of America (ADAA) states in an online article, 'Physical Activity Reduces Stress', that exercise can 'decrease overall levels of tension, elevate and stabilize mood, improve sleep, and improve self-esteem. Even five minutes of aerobic exercise can stimulate anti-anxiety effects.'

Overall, exercise is a great relaxer, and worry seems to ebb when we get active.

Diet

Stress affects our appetite, and when we're feeling anxious, we can swing from completely losing our appetite to comfort eating. Anxiety often feels like a knot in the stomach and leaves you feeling on edge, which makes it hard to digest food. Seek to understand which foods you digest easily, and eat regular meals that are part of a balanced diet. Eating well is a simple way to shift one area that directly impacts our anxiety levels. It is easy to monitor the foods we eat, understand how they affect us and focus on having the right proportions. We do not want to be struggling with food when we already feel on edge.

Caffeine

Caffeine is one of the worst things we can drink if we are feeling panicky; it is a stimulant that can easily trigger anxiety. It arouses the nervous system, increasing our heart rate and leaving us restless. Consequently, it is difficult to distinguish between what the caffeine has fuelled and what our body is actually going through on its own accord. (This overlap is similar to that of anxiety and excitement in 2.3, *Do Not Live in Fear*.) Caffeine is also proven to negatively influence sleep, clarity of thought and adrenaline levels. To sum up – quit caffeine and in all likelihood your anxiety levels will reduce.

Drugs and alcohol

As GP'ers, we live hard-and-fast lifestyles and are constantly trying to keep up with those around us. Most of our social life is focused on Friday and Saturday nights, which are fuelled with drugs – including cigarettes – and alcohol. We look to these substance-filled evenings for a release from the routine of the working week; it is a coping strategy that numbs our frustrations and anxiety. In a moment, it can seem like a wonderful idea to gain more confidence and join in with the crowd, but doing so can lead to far more harm than good.

Stimulants and depressants result in a chemical imbalance that can impact how we think and behave under pressure. Drugs and alcohol ultimately leave us feeling irritable and sensitive, and being temperamental can dominate our interactions with others. They impact the way that we think and react, particularly as their abuse can lead to paranoia and anxiety. They allow the negative voices of our Saboteurs (chapter 4.2) to take over our minds by repeating limiting and self-destructive phrases. On a more tangible level, we are all too aware of the health risks that these substances can have on our body.

Sleep

Lack of sleep influences our mood and, most significantly, how we deal with our anxiety. In their article 'The Complex Relationship between Sleep, Depression & Anxiety', the National Sleep Foundation says that 'when you don't get the 7-9 hours of quality sleep you need, it can heavily influence your outlook on life, energy level, motivation, and emotions'.

Sleep has unbelievable benefits, helping us feel happier and better prepared to face the day. Our days are already speckled with moments of anxiety, so we do not need to add fatigue to the worry. Without sleep, these moments become magnified, and it is possible for us to spiral downwards far quicker than if we had slept well. Let's put ourselves in the best position to combat anxiety with a full night's sleep.

Also remember that anxiety can take a lot out of us physically, emotionally and mentally. Our bodies can feel tense and unrelaxed, which produces negative emotions. We need sleep to refuel and carry out mental processing.

Jump into Action

+ *Make it flow*

Always have water handy by using a proper water bottle. You can even get a see-through one and write an inspirational quote on the outside to get you fuelled up. If increasing your water intake is a struggle, create a game with a friend, partner or colleague in which for two weeks, you jot down the benefits you have felt from drinking plenty of water.

Whenever you are feeling particularly anxious, tell yourself that it is crucial that you drink water. Taking regular and small sips is key.

+ *Shift your butt!*

Get creative and try out a range of activities, anything from skipping to Pilates, ballet to boxing. Many people find yoga works for them, but don't get stressed if it doesn't work for you. Instead, try a range of sports, and you might find swimming, running or trampolining suits you better. Don't feel pressured to find a release in what others do; keep searching to find your best outlet.

After each activity, notice how you feel. Create a workout diary where you can write down what you are trying, how it made you feel, how your anxiety felt on a scale of 1–10 and lessons you have learnt. You can also diarise your workouts so there is no escape! Commit and follow through.

Also make a poster that labels your reasons for exercising. For example, 'Be Less Stressed & Control My Anxiety' or 'Sleep Well & Be Happier'. Now put this poster somewhere you can see it regularly. If you are feeling a little sluggish or downbeat, it will be a wonderful reminder to get you moving again.

Finally, if you are caught in a meeting with surplus energy or feeling restless at the end of the day, consider the following movements and exercises:

- Form fists with your hands under the table and squeeze for five to ten seconds, then release. Stretch out your fingers fully.
- Tense your legs. Uncross them, put your feet flat on the floor and then squeeze them. Curl your toes and hold for five seconds.
- Release your jaw and wiggle it around.
- Breathe deeply using 7-7-7 (chapter 1.2).
- Change your tone and pace of voice. Use your energy to spice up your delivery or slow it down and see the impact on you and those around you.
- Stand tall and relaxed with shoulders back. Be alert but have a 'softness' in your body (chapter 1.4).
- Go for a light stroll, slowing things down and taking in what is around you (chapter 5.1).

+ *You are what you eat*

Keep your food clean and a variety of colours. As mentioned, work out which foods move easily through your system, and if necessary, keep a food journal to help. In particular, cut out as much sugar as you can as it spikes your blood sugar levels, which can make you feel more jittery. Every time you feel the need to reach for a quick energy surge or sugary treat, ask yourself, 'Is this going to reduce my anxiety or fuel it?' Finally, consider eating small amounts often so that if a bout of anxiety hits and you lose your appetite, you have enough in reserve to get through it. Come up with a food plan to ensure you are eating a balanced diet of foods that work for you. Try it for a week and note your progress.

+ *Go decaf!*

If you find the taste of caffeinated coffee delicious, it is not an excuse. You can get excellent decaf coffees nowadays pretty much everywhere.

Start with replacing one caffeinated drink with one decaf drink each day. If that is too hard, go for once a week. Over time, decrease your daily caffeine intake until you don't need it anymore. You will realise you are far calmer without it. After you have weaned yourself off it, notice how your sleep, your mood and your anxiety have been impacted. If you need to, tell people what you are doing and ask for their support.

+ *Choose natural highs*

First of all, become honest with how much you consume each week. Clarity around how much you consume, as well as when and why, is the first step in gaining awareness. Write down in your journal how many cigarettes you smoke, how many units of alcohol you consume and, if you take drugs, what drugs, how much and how often.

Then jot down your feelings and reactions to the figures you have written. Notice timings or potential trends that cause you to reach for a cigarette, drug or glass of alcohol. See if there are any cyclical triggers that lead you to that point. Is there a particular group of friends that you indulge with? Do you substitute it for negative feelings? Think about their true impact individually and ask, 'What do they actually give me?' or 'What am I avoiding?'

Clearly using none is the optimal goal here, but reducing what you do use is better than nothing. First, talk to friends, family or help lines to gain support. If any of them have gone through a similar process of cutting back, then get their tips as to what worked and what did not, and use them for support (reread the chapter *You Are Not Alone* if needed).

Likewise, your friends are the sum of those around you (read more in 3.1, *Radiators & Drainers*). If you surround yourself with people who enjoy partying late on a Saturday night, question whether these 'friends' are the right friends for you, particularly at this time in your life. Imagine you are on the outside looking in at each relationship; how healthy it is for you right now? At this moment, with all you have on your plate, is it truly benefitting you? If yes, then great. If no, consider hanging out with people who are not involved in these antics. If there is a situation where you think friends will be drinking, smoking or taking drugs, then contemplate avoiding this space for now. Remember, these substances do nothing to help you remain calm and level-headed.

Ask a reliable friend to hold you accountable and suggest that you come up with goals together. Brainstorm activities and rewards that could replace any of the substances. For example, if you wake up feeling fresh on a Saturday morning, you could reward yourself and acknowledge how that state benefits you. Think about how you can use the time you would otherwise be spending with a hangover. We all need more time, so cut out the stimulants to provide you with this. At the very least, you will waste less of your time feeling anxious.

+ *Have sweet dreams*
Here are some ideas for sleeping better, in no particular order. You may need to try them multiple times, as a one-hit wonder tip might not work for a whole host of reasons on another day.

This list is not restrictive, so brainstorm other ideas that might benefit you.

- First things first: stop worrying that you cannot sleep. This sounds obvious, but literally saying, 'Stop! I am not going to worry about this,' can give some respite.
- Take a hot bath. Use bath salts, bath oil, bubbles or nothing – play around and see if it has any bearing.
- Go for a short stroll before you go to sleep; ideally get outside in nature for a relaxed amble.
- Cancel the diary for the next two weeks. Carve out time for you and put yourself at the centre.
- Get some really nice bed sheets in a soothing, neutral colour that makes you feel calm.
- Write down a schedule for the next day so you have a clear action plan as to what you would like to achieve tomorrow.
- Repaint or redecorate your room for calmer surroundings.
- Exercise regularly to release the extra energy.
- Practise a digital detox – no phones, laptops or television before or in bed.
- Get an alarm clock (or two if you are worried about missing one!).
- Get a night light if you are afraid of the dark.
- Drink a cup of herbal tea before bed.
- Listen to relaxing music – classical or acoustic – while you wind down.
- Clean your sheets regularly.
- Avoid watching a high-energy, aggressive or dramatic program or film before going to sleep.
- Use a weighted blanket.
- Take deep breaths.
- Do a short stint of mindfulness/meditation.
- Buy bedclothes that you feel comfortable and good in.
- Dim the lights in your room before going to bed.

- Always make your bed in the morning so it is ready and fresh when you come back in the evening.
- Eat uncomplicated food, and ideally eat earlier in the evening.
- Try to go to sleep and wake up at a similar time each day so that your body can get into a pattern; set a regular routine to be followed every day, including the weekends.
- Read a book before going to bed.
- Talk to someone you trust to run through any worries that are on your mind so that they don't build up at night.
- Eat a banana or an oatcake if you cannot sleep.
- In the day, try to keep calm and stress-free; stop rushing and slow down.
- Do a head-to-toe relaxation by clenching different parts of your body as hard as you can. Starting from your head, clench your eyes, your teeth, your jaw, your shoulder, your forearm, your hands, etc. Work your way down your body and tighten each part for five seconds before releasing. Or start from your extremities and work inwards to your core. If you still feel tense at the end, keep repeating.
- Imagine a calming waterfall washing over your body.
- Visualise a place where sleep comes easy, and 'go' to this place when you go to your room.
- Relax at different moments throughout the day to take the pressure off the night-time. Perhaps take a nap (or at least shut your eyes) in the afternoon.
- Focus on your anxiety and be present with it; do not try to fight it.
- Cut out *all* alcohol, or if you can't, at least cut it down.
- Make your bedroom a tech-free zone – no phones, iPads, laptops, etc.
- If you have a big pitch for work the next day, keep the notes somewhere close by so you feel like you can reach them if needs be. Put them under your pillow or far away

from your bedroom – whatever works!
- Keep a notepad by your bed to jot down anything whirring through your mind.
- Remind yourself that at some point, you will drift off.
- If all else fails, count sheep!

All these suggestions can also be implemented if you wake up in the middle of the night worrying. Try different ones and see what works.

My Experience

When I experienced severe panic attacks, I found that I needed to step back from everything. Prior to this I did most things in excess and struggled to find a good balance. So although this chapter is not scientifically driven, from my experience the tweaks that I made here greatly reduced how anxious I felt.

First, I stopped drinking all caffeine. Although it was hard at the time, I have never looked back. I sleep better, feel better and don't have spikes of anxiety. To replace it, I drink lots of water and often try to take little sips to stay hydrated (particularly when I am feeling anxious, so that I don't feel like I have lots of water sloshing around in me). I found when I first started having panic attacks, even drinking made me feel queasy, so the little-and-often approach has worked well for me. This principle also applied to food – smaller amounts and easier-to-digest foods since eating big meals made me feel sick and more anxious. It almost felt as though my body went into panic mode as the digestion process was too much to handle on top of the anxiety I was experiencing. So, I had little bites throughout the day to ensure that I had enough energy to get through a panic attack.

I also cut out cigarettes and all alcohol – the positive effects of which are all over the Internet, so I do not need to preach. Today, I drink far less and I am also more aware of what my body can handle; for example, wine wakes me up in the night and makes me feel anxious as I worry about nothing and everything, so I don't drink it anymore.

And finally sleep – wow, the importance of sleep. I have always been a light sleeper, as I often have nightmares and find that I worry in the middle of the night. I am also scared of the dark. So, I realised that I needed to set myself up for good sleep using techniques to deal with whatever the night brings. I use all of them at different times, but one of the best is keeping a notepad by my bed so I can write down anything on my mind. By getting it out of my head and onto paper, I feel a weight lifting from my shoulders – anything from buying milk in the morning to putting together that important document for a client.

Go for It

Think about your body as a whole. By following some of the advice in this chapter, we can better balance our emotional state and therefore be better equipped to balance our anxiety. Some small tweaks are guaranteed to lead to a healthier and happier you!

3. Circle of Influence

No road is long with good company.
– Turkish Proverb

3.1 Radiators & Drainers
3.2 Masks
3.3 Boundaries
3.4 Safe Person
3.5 Build a Support Network

3.1 Radiators & Drainers

It isn't the mountains ahead to climb that wear you out, it's the pebble in your shoe.
– Muhammad Ali

Snapshot

It is said that we are the average of the people around us. If we surround ourselves with brilliant, uplifting people we are likely to have a positive outlook on life. If we surround ourselves with negative people, it results in a pessimistic attitude. Our relationships have a profound impact on our lives. If they are going well, our experiences are more positive and happy. When things are not going swimmingly, we feel unhappy and a little lost. It is important to have the right people around us – they will help us grow and support us even in the toughest of times. We must choose Radiators and not Drainers.

A Radiator is just that – someone who radiates happiness, positivity and optimism. When we spend time in the company of a Radiator, we feel uplifted, happier and 'filled up'. Being in their presence changes how we think and feel. Radiators might not be carbon copies of us – they might be people who challenge us, or have different views and opinions.

On the other hand, a Drainer is what it says on the tin – someone who drains us of confidence. They get a kick out of sabotaging us and leave us feeling emotionally and physically exhausted. As they delight in failure and rarely look for the positives, all feels heavy and exhausting in their company.

Importance to GP'ers

We need to distinguish between these two types of people and stay in the company of Radiators. Our lives will change for the better – everything will be more exciting, positive and forward thinking. Just picture finishing a long and tough day at work. You can decide between meeting someone who will build you up and make you feel great, or you could meet with a Drainer and let them take away your positivity. It's a no-brainer.

Don't let the Drainers win. Don't let them drag you down to their level, and instead surround yourself with Radiators who truly want you to be the best possible version of yourself.

In light of all this, we need to ensure that we are not becoming a Drainer and instead become what we want to attract. Absolutely have good friends to air problems with, but always try to be positive and look for the good in things. Attempt to get through evenings with friends without slamming other people or being mean toward others. It never makes us feel better about ourselves in the long run, so avoid it altogether. Those who are positive attract like-minded people, so be the Radiator instead. Make others feel important and truly listen to them – they are worthy of your time. Appreciate them for all their faults and praise them when they are magnificent.

Jump into Action

+ *Decide between Radiators and Drainers*
This is a great exercise to become aware of who you are surrounding yourself with and the circles of contacts you operate within.

Go through the people you know and write them all down into groups – falling under overarching categories, such as university friends, immediate family, work colleagues, mentors, etc. Next to each person, write down whether they are Radiators or Drainers. Then ask yourself:

- Is one group predominantly people I have a 'surface' relationship with?
- Is another group focused on one sex?
- Is another unit quite small?
- Despite knowing these people for many years, are they actually good friends to me?
- Who can I really rely on?
- Is there anyone who is less trustworthy?
- What else do I notice, or what stands out about the circles?

Nothing is right or wrong here; you are simply getting a bird's eye view.

+ *Take it to the next level*

Now go through each group. What do you notice? Perhaps label the overriding title of the group – i.e., are you in the company of Drainers or Radiators here?

Next, examine the people who sit within each group. Be truthful with yourself and think about the impact they have on you. When you are in their company, how do you feel? If you are unsure, do not mark Drainer or Radiator by their name. Meet them in the coming weeks, and when you come away, ask yourself how you feel about them. Did you have a positive experience, or was there a sense that you had to 'endure' your time together in some way?

+ *Look ahead*

Once you have reviewed your list, plan to see the people who have an upbeat and positive mindset. Schedule and spend time with them; get in touch now with one Radiator to set something up.

+ *Positivity is the best policy*

Now flip it over to you – adopt the Radiator mindset. Write down a list of all your positive qualities. If you are struggling, ask your friends what they value about you, and then add to it the qualities of a Radiator (or what you would think them to be). Now pop this list in a place where you can see it regularly. Remind yourself daily of all the attributes you wish to uphold.

My Experience

Radiators and Drainers is a concept my Mum taught me from a young age. The image speaks to me as I imagine Radiators literally radiating warmth, light and energy. I always aspire to be this and continue surrounding myself with mostly Radiators.

When I am feeling down or anxious, checking in with the type of people I am hanging out with quite often shows that I have spent more time with Drainers, and I just need to flip it.

Go for It

To reduce your anxiety and enjoy life more, eliminate the Drainers, surround yourself with Radiators and be a Radiator.

3.2 Masks

Courage is like a muscle. We strengthen it by use.
– Ruth Gordon

This chapter will not be for everyone, but have a read anyway and see if it holds any pearls of wisdom for you. It is focused on awareness and understanding current behaviours, rather than quick fixes.

Snapshot

Masks are the personas that we put on for different or even all parts of our lives. A mask feeds on fear and becomes a role to play, particularly if the public self is happy yet the private self is going through hell. As we constantly battle to keep the mask on, our anxiety can hit an all-time high.

Masks hide our authentic self, by making it difficult to be able to speak up and be seen. They are limiting and suffocating, and they can be exhausting to maintain.

As humans, we have a profound desire to be accepted by those around us. Yet masks take it to another level, which is unsustainable. We need to start being honest with ourselves and with those around us ... and we can begin by dropping the masks.

Importance to GP'ers

Negative masks can be detrimental. They do not help us bypass anxiety and get through tough situations; instead, keeping up the façade that all is okay leaves us exhausted and overwhelmed. For example, if we are trying to be an extrovert but we are actually an introvert, it can be dangerous to don the extrovert mask. We will not be true to ourselves, and living a fake life can be damaging and demoralising. There is no doubt that our anxiety levels will increase every time we put on a mask.

Jump into Action

+ *Test out the mask*

Try putting on an actual mask (or recall a time you wore one) and notice how you feel. What are you aware of? Think about the physicality of it; it can often block your line of sight, make you feel claustrophobic and obstruct dialogue.

Now try on different types of masks. Does your perspective change with different ones? Do some give you a positive feeling – as though you are invisible and can do anything? Don't judge your emotions, whether positive or negative.

+ *Realise you're masking your emotions*

Consider what masks you wear and their characteristics. Question what triggers the need for different masks for *you*. For example, you might have a mask that shows you are keeping on top of everything at work. And you might notice that this mask becomes particularly heavy when you discuss ongoing project updates with your boss.

Take a moment to draw a quick sketch of the masks that you wear. You might be surprised how quickly the masks appear to you. Draw, or write down a description of, as many as you can come up with.

+ *Spot the difference*

When it comes to your personas, or masks, it is important to distinguish between what you want to hold on to and what you want to be rid of. Write down the key characteristics of your masks and focus on the differences. What is significant about when they arise? How do they serve you in that moment? Do they have your best interests at heart? How can you regain control and make sure you do not put on a mask?

If it helps, buy a mask you can put on as a reminder of what you do not want to do and how it feels to wear one.

My Experience

When I feel on the back foot and insecure, I often put on a mask of confidence to pretend everything is okay. I have good intentions, but in reality, it comes across as desperate and false as I try to show that I am 'nailing it'. It is inauthentic, and although in the moment it feels like a better approach, afterwards I am appalled that I put on a show. It is important that I am aware of this mask and when I like to put it on so that I can catch myself doing it more easily.

I also have physically put on masks to play around, and the physical impact is immediate – I feel panicky, restricted and claustrophobic, and my speech is hindered. This ensures that the message hits home!

Go for It

Be curious about the masks you put on. In doing so, you will increase your self-awareness and build your emotional resilience. Remember, you have choices.

3.3 Boundaries

I am not what happened to me, I am what I choose to become.
– Carl Jung

Snapshot

Boundaries are important, as they are clear definitions of where and what our limitations are. They let us – and those around us – understand the fine line between what we are okay with and what we are not okay with. By defining these restrictions and communicating them, we are left feeling empowered and in control. Boundaries also lead to more honest and open relationships, as those around us know where they stand.

Boundaries often represent our values and indicate what we attach importance to in our lives. When boundaries are crossed, it is usually negatively charged as our values have been walked all over. As a result, boundaries can be created when a value has been stepped on and we realise that we wish to honour a belief that is central to us. From here we can understand what our boundaries are and communicate them to those around us, particularly people close to us such as family members, as they will be repeatedly impacted by them.

Boundaries can be difficult to set, and it is often a trial-and-error exercise to work out our limits. They can also change quickly and shape-shift seamlessly, so we need to remember to constantly revisit them.

Importance to GP'ers

Getting clarity on and defining our boundaries allows us to be aware of our limitations, as well as making it clear to ourselves where the line cannot be crossed – both professionally and personally. Most significantly, it lets others know when they are pushing us too far (or perhaps at times not quite enough). When they have been breached, communicating our boundaries can lead to a simple discussion: e.g., 'As I mentioned to you previously, being late is a non-negotiable for me. I am really disappointed that you are late.'

The ability to clearly communicate our boundaries to those closest to us is a skill. Yet conveying our limitations in a crystal-clear, assertive way is necessary. From there, we can honour them and not be swayed by other people's biases.

Jump into Action

+ *Know that clarity is key*

First things first: understand your boundaries. Note the times that make you feel under pressure, and be inquisitive as to what you are feeling in that particular moment.

Take a moment to reflect in a quiet, calm place. When was the last time that you were frustrated? What happened? What values did the person step on? Jot down what comes up.

Another approach is to draw a big circle on a piece of paper. Inside the circle, write down or draw symbols to represent your values (e.g., loyalty, honesty, consistency, freedom, kindness, etc.). You could even draw an inner circle to put your core values in, those that you hold in the highest regard, such as love, dependability and commitment. The outside rim represents your boundaries, and the clearer you get on where they lie, the better. Now consider *how* you are going to honour these values every day.

+ *Be honest*

Be proactive and speak openly with those closest to you about what is most important to you. This will leave you on the front foot.

And if there is a time or a specific example of someone stepping on your boundaries, then be prepared to openly address it with them. Before confronting the person, centre yourself – consider breathing deep (7-7-7 as you learned in chapter 1.2), and write down the reasons you want to raise the concern. You should see enough valid points to make you feel sure-footed as you go into these conversations.

My Experience

I am much more aware of my boundaries now than I ever have been, but it is an area that I must continue to focus on and develop, as boundaries shift and change constantly. Some of my biggest boundaries are around time, transparency and kindness. I hate it when people are late, lie or are mean to each other. To better communicate these, I must stretch myself out of my comfort zone to have those conversations. Although they feel hard in the short term, that level of honesty benefits me in the long term.

Go for It

Boundaries are hard as they can change. However, the clearer you get on where yours are right now, the easier things become. By setting clear guidelines and protecting yourself and what is important to you, the more likely it is for anxiety to take a breather.

3.4 Safe Person

It is during our darkest moments that we must focus to see the light.
– Aristotle

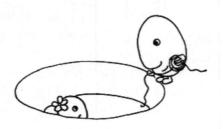

Snapshot

When anxiety takes over, it is overwhelming and disorientating. As we spiral out of control, we land in a place so dark that we cannot see what is in front of us, and all we have is a sinking feeling. As our anxiety bubbles up, we get more disconnected from life, disconnected from others and disconnected from ourselves.

In that moment, rational thoughts escape us, and we have no clarity of mind. We need a 'Safe Person' – someone who knows us really well to help us feel reconnected to ourselves. Normally we suffer in silence as we think that we can handle it and feel too embarrassed to ask for help. However, a Safe Person is essential in order to help us get rid of anxiety. They know who we truly are. People say that when they are anxious, they 'do not feel themselves', that they are 'out of character' or that they have 'lost who they are'. A Safe Person can remind us of the 'before anxiety' version of ourselves.

The Safe Person should be someone we trust implicitly – a family member, a partner, an excellent friend, a great colleague, a coach, a therapist. The vital traits of our Safe Person must be honesty, trustworthiness, discretion, openness, non-judgementalism, kindness and understanding. The list can be extended as necessary.

If you cannot think of anyone who falls into this category, this might be a moment for you to rethink your relationships with those around you (reread the chapter *Radiators & Drainers*). It is important to surround ourselves with people who embody these characteristics and have a positive influence on our lives.

Importance to GP'ers

A Safe Person can help us keep our feet on the ground in moments of panic and overwhelming pressure. They can be the first port of call to support us and try to understand what is going on. Their help and encouragement in those disconnected moments is so valuable, as it can change how we are reacting by offering a comforting voice. Moreover, their familiarity and reasoning can be calming when everything else seems to be running away from us.

Having a Safe Person allows us to open up to our support network. It will help us realise that people will accept our anxiety and that many others have gone through something similar. By being open and honest, we might well be surprised at what comes back.

Jump into Action

+ *Hunt them down!*

First, identify a Safe Person. Think about those who surround you, and identify one person who will be able to take on this important role. From there, open up with your Safe Person and ask them to support you. Get them to understand what you are going through and how they can help.

+ Be specific

Tell your Safe Person what you need; in particular, what you need in the moment when anxiety takes over. It is key to understand what happens to you when panic rules and you lose rational thoughts. By looking at and learning from previous experiences of anxious moments, you can recognise what actions, words and thoughts have helped you calm down. Perhaps you can write cue cards (chapter 1.5) for your Safe Person to read to you when you are in an anxiety-filled state. Ideas could be:

- Remind me to breathe deeply, 7-7-7.
- Tell me about your surroundings – what can you smell, see or hear?
- Don't forget to roll your shoulders to release the tension, and then try and drop them.
- Try loosening your jaw by wiggling it around.
- Find a safe place to go to now and be away from others, such as a meeting room out of the office environment or a nearby park.

Now create reminders (sticky notes, phone alarms, a picture of your Safe Person nearby) that will trigger you to get in touch and pick up the phone when you feel the panic escalating.

+ Adjust as time passes

In time, you can review the process and tweak your relationship with your Safe Person. In particular, consider decreasing your dependency on them. As you build strength, you can begin to self-manage your anxiety until a separate part of you can step into the role of the Safe Person. This means that when going through a panic attack, you are still able to access a part of you that can talk rationally. (For more on this concept, check out chapter 4.1, *Connect with Your Best Self*.) This can be developed as you become more aware of how you react to different scenarios and also increasingly conscious of what you truly need in those spiralling anxious moments.

+ *Heed this word of warning*
You should not become dependent on your Safe Person, and you cannot fall into the trap of calling them ten times a day. The Safe Person should be relied on only when things are truly escalating into panic. The rest of the book gives you tips and ideas about how to conquer anxiety, so remember that your Safe Person is merely *one* resource you can use alongside other tools you accrue. Keep an ongoing and open discussion with your Safe Person to ensure that you do not become dependent on them and instead are building your own strength.

+ *Kindness goes in circles*
On a side note, remember to support your Safe Person too. It doesn't need to be big, but acknowledgement is key. Say thank you, send them a note or give your time to listen to them. This ensures that both sides feel like it is a balanced relationship and no one is taking advantage of the other.

My Experience

My number one Safe Person is my husband. I call him whenever I am feeling anxious, and he knows how to calm me down and say the best things to me. His encouragement has evolved over time, but essentially he acts like my biggest fan, believing in me fully. It was hard for me to learn to rely on someone else, to be open about my panic and accept that I was struggling. Regardless, I couldn't have gotten through it without him.

I also make a conscious effort to ensure that my dependency does not become lopsided, so that I am there for him too and I acknowledge and thank him for his help.

Go for It

Do not try to conquer anxiety alone, as you will dig yourself into a dark hole. Even if you are not feeling strong enough to open up to friends and family, I would advise you to confide in that one Safe Person who can support you when things escalate.

3.5 Build a Support Network

Dig the well before you are thirsty.
– Chinese Proverb

Snapshot

Building connections is what life is all about. By connecting with others, we get a sense of belonging and a feeling of self-worth.

Our support network can consist of all sorts of people – positive Radiators, friends, colleagues and family members. But it can also extend to people outside of our 'inner core' who can reassure and inspire us; for example, a mentor, someone we met at an event, a coach or perhaps someone we were introduced to. We can count on this wide range of people to support us in times of anxiety. By building a network that can genuinely encourage and empower us, we can begin to move powerfully forward.

Also remember that every relationship consists of a bit of give and take. It is like a waltz where one dancer needs to have their time to shine whilst the other supports them, and vice versa. In the same way, we should ensure that our relationships are in balance across all aspects of our lives. When the dance falls out of sync, the dancers are out of kilter and the partnership fails to work. Therefore, let us build a solid support network of people who can dance the same dance and catch us when we slip up. These people should also understand what is important to us, such as our boundaries (chapter 3.3) and our goals. This means that they can help us move ahead to what we truly want to achieve.

Importance to GP'ers

A strong network around us makes us better people and gives us a greater sense of belonging and purpose. Moreover, we will feel inspired to achieve our goals rather than let anxiety rule.

Our support network can be there to offer advice and help us deal with any instability in our lives. In particular, those outside our immediate family and friends can offer us unbiased and non-judgemental advice. It is important to have a varied group of people so that we can gather new perspectives and see things from a different angle.

For example, a coach will be on our side and not criticise our decisions, instead fully believing that we know the right path forward. Likewise, a mentor will be able to offer guidance from their own experiences and the lessons they have learnt. Having a mentor or a coach we admire will ensure that we are constantly striving to be better people, and they will also help us avoid pitfalls by functioning as sounding boards. By holding us to account, they will put us at a significant advantage over our peers and stop us from procrastinating.

We must ensure that we are building the right network of Radiators (chapter 3.1) – with people we admire, respect and look up to. Often a great way to succeed in our goals is to support those around us in accomplishing theirs.

Here is the takeaway: by creating a strong, diverse network to support, inspire and motivate us, we will build the confidence and clarity needed to achieve our goals.

Jump into Action

+ *Build your network*

Take a piece of paper and write down the names of people you surround yourself with (you may want to build on the list from chapter 3.1). Then, jot down which category they fall into; for example, friend, colleague, coach, family, etc. Ask yourself whether each individual is clear on how they can support you.

Next, think bigger and consider what you want from your support network. What do you expect from them, and what can you give back to them? Write down these answers as well.

+ *Variety is the spice of life*

Now get curious about what type of person would add a different perspective or a different energy to your network. Conceivably, there is someone you admire who could be an excellent mentor to you. Perhaps there is a coach you have come across who would improve your confidence and clarity. Is there someone you met at a meeting (through work or on a personal level) with whom you established a good rapport? Think about this person and consider what they do. How do they do it so well? What characteristics do they display that you would benefit from? How can you get them into your life?

+ *Grow it*

Once you have built your support network, make sure you develop it. It will take time and energy, so prioritise what, and who, is most important to you. And remember to be supportive to those who support you – whether a loyal friend, colleague or family member – the relationship should be a balanced dance together.

+ *Speak up*

As with your Safe Person in the last chapter, tell the people in your network that they are important to you and how you specifically appreciate their support. Again, a simple word of thanks goes a long way, so be grateful for those around you and express your thanks. Even a small gesture can have a huge impact on their continued support.

My Experience

I continue to build a diverse and interesting support network around me. The range of people and personalities ensures that I can go to different people for different topics or energies that I am looking for. For example, sometimes I want someone who has specific experience in a topic and has a calm and peaceful outlook, whereas the next moment I might want to interact with someone who is fired up and task focused. I am always working with a coach, too, so that I have an external and non-judgemental sounding board. I also like mentors off whom I can bounce ideas and get advice, although it is not always easy to find good ones. In addition, interacting with a range of people keeps me grounded and gives me fresh perspectives. Once I push past the initial anxiety and out of my comfort zone, I find that nine times out of ten, I feel less anxious and happier.

Go for It

Build a support network of people who are on your side and will encourage you to operate at your best. Then acknowledge and thank them for their help.

4. Your Best Self vs. Saboteurs

You can't let people set your agenda in life.
– Warren Buffett

4.1 Connect with Your Best Self
4.2 Saboteurs
4.3 Create a Dialogue with Your Saboteurs
4.4 Non-Judgement

4.1 Connect with Your Best Self

Wherever you go, you take yourself with you.
– Neil Gaiman

Snapshot

Different people call the concept different things: superhero, inner leader, captain, internal CEO, champion or idol. Whatever term you give it, the principle is the same: our Best Self is the wise and compassionate part of us that is always right and helps to lead us through our lives. In the toughest of times, it believes in us entirely and knows how to find the best route forward, even if the path ahead looks challenging and blocked. By connecting to our Best Self, we get the strength and clarity to move forward, even if things seem impossible at first glance.

Most importantly, the Best Self is able to stand up to our Saboteurs (chapter 4.2). It is able to stamp out the negative and self-limiting monologue that runs wild in our heads and replace it with a far more constructive and wise perspective.

Importance to GP'ers

Connecting with our Best Self reminds us that we have infinite resources already in us. It represents someone or something that is continuously on our side and has our best interests at heart. When we feel particularly anxious and backed up against a wall, it can be a relief to know that there is a resource deep inside us that is kind and compassionate. It is not cruel; it does not criticise what we do. Our Best Self offers us a safe haven where we are not judged and where we know that we can, and we will, move forward.

Our Best Self can be called upon when we are faced with a scary situation, such as public speaking, a date or an important meeting at work. It will give us more confidence and strength to get through it – not just surviving it, but actually doing it well and even, dare I say it, enjoying it.

Jump into Action

+ *Connect with your Best Self*

Take a moment to connect with your Best Self. Pick a day

when your anxiety levels are feeling lower and perhaps when something positive has occurred that you feel particularly proud of.

Now take some deep breaths using 7-7-7 several times. Then close your eyes and get comfortable. From this quieter space, really connect and listen to your gut (chapter 2.5). Tune in to the part of you that knows your strengths and talents and has complete clarity on the best way forward. Everyone has this power within, so just take a moment to not only find it, but also connect with it.

Now start to give your Best Self a physical form in your mind. Remember, your Best Self can take on multiple representations at different times and in different situations. What does each representation look like? Go into the detail of how they come across. Are they an object, an animal or a human? What are they wearing or what colour are their eyes? What else do you notice about their appearance? Do they smell of anything? What do they say? How do they act? Do they have a catchphrase? How can they add value to you in a particular moment? What name can you give them? Keep questioning to develop your vision and make them come alive.

Imagine you are drawing them (or actually do) for even better detail on every aspect. The clarity you get now will benefit you later on when life feels tough and you need to access them.

+ *Create a talisman*

Think of a way that you can represent your Best Self – is there an object that perfectly represents a particular manifestation of your Best Self? Could you write a poem? Perhaps draw out what these representations look like? There might be a song you could listen to that encapsulates all that they stand for. Play around with it and find what works for you. Once you have a talisman, keep it close to you so it can remind you of your Best Self.

+ *Get easy access*

Now brainstorm how you can easily access your Best Self. How will you know that you need to call upon them? How can you remember to access them? What can their knowledge and wisdom give you in that moment? Could you create a reminder? Pop a sticky note on the mirror? Save your screensaver as the image it represents? Play the piece of music that reminds you of them every morning?

Remember to use this resource in the future. Build up your relationship so that you can easily call on them when you need to. For the next two weeks, try to think about your Best Self at least once a day, however anxious or calm you are feeling. Then build on that number. After all, why wouldn't you want more access to this strength, wisdom and confidence?

If you are struggling to connect with this part of you, just leave it – take a breather for a couple of days. If you are feeling particularly anxious, try to hold off until things have eased a little and you feel more in control. It is okay for it not to come immediately for you. Focus on another chapter in the book for now and revisit at a time that feels right.

My Experience

I absolutely love my Best Self and have a clear vision of myself when I am operating at my optimal state. I see a strong, confident and powerful animal. She brings me strength when I most need it, always knows the best way forward and has wisdom that I can call upon. When I am particularly struggling, I usually am disconnected from my animal. In those moments, I just need to remind myself to use her. She is an excellent resource, and I try to keep her at the forefront of my mind so that I can call upon her with ease. I even have screensavers (many over the years) that represent her, and I have a couple of little sculptures that I often carry around with me in my bag to serve as reminders.

I hope that you access and use your Best Self. I've heard of all sorts of Best Selves, including, but most certainly not limited to, wise men, trees, animals, bits of nature, older selves and younger selves. For me, this is one of the most important concepts in this book.

Go for It

Your Best Self is always there and always a part of you. Use its strength and wisdom to your advantage.

4.2 Saboteurs

Every time I overcome an obstacle, it feels like success. Sometimes the biggest ones are in our head – the saboteurs that tell us we can't.
– Lupita Nyong'o

Snapshot

Depending on who we speak to, the concept of the Saboteur is a negative or less positive voice that can be described in many ways: gremlin, the chatterbox, an annoying internal flatmate, the judge, the inner critic, an inner voice or a critical voice (to name just a few!). These pesky good-for-nothings represent our worries and fears. Saboteurs literally sabotage us. They are the voices in our head that hold us back and take control of our lives. Saboteurs are dangerous as they make us question our self-worth and subsequently lead us to believe that we are never good enough.

Saboteurs shape-shift and disguise their voices through our normal thoughts. They create catchphrases, images and films from our deepest fears which have a profound impact on our way of thinking. Our Saboteurs express our self-limiting beliefs and suck us into their power until we believe what they are telling us. The easiest way to spot a Saboteur is by the language it uses – a lot of *should*s and *have to*s. Phrases that surface are along the lines of, 'I have to do the presentation to please my boss' or 'I should go to this party to meet new people.' And, 'I must be unlovable,' 'You should go faster' or 'You should be better at this.'

With Saboteurs, when we tune into the nonsense of what they are saying, we understand that we are merely the observer. We are on the *outside*, observing what our Saboteurs are saying. As a result, we have control over whether we listen to them and if we want to get sucked into their way of thinking. We have a choice about how we want to interact with our Saboteurs. Often just by noticing what is going on and not getting involved in the detail of what they are saying, we can build our strength to deal with them.

Importance to GP'ers

We are not alone; every GP'er will have a Saboteur of some description, guaranteed. Despite Saboteurs being hard to define, we need to get a good handle on who or what they are to us individually, as everyone is different. Only then can we deal with them effectively. Saboteurs are crafty rascals who can change their voice and personality depending on the situation. They know our weak spots and how to make us believe the worst in ourselves. When these creatures control our lives, it becomes exhausting and limiting.

Awareness is key, and by having our Saboteurs in sight and separating their voice from our normal thoughts, we can begin to move forward with confidence and make better decisions.

We can allow ourselves to minimise self-doubt and be the best version of ourselves, without anything holding us back. Moreover, as we listen to a kinder voice in our heads – our Best Self (chapter 4.1) – our anxiety will subside.

We do not need to be loyal and believe our Saboteurs – they haven't benefitted us in the past, so what are we going to gain now? Remember that we are just the people noticing the chatter, and it is the saboteurs babbling away on a stream of negative thoughts. We are separate from them. Let's create some distance from our Saboteurs and watch them objectively, by viewing them from the *outside*.

Jump into Action

+ *Create a profile*
Know that your Saboteurs will try to deceive you. To stop their trickery, we can create a profile of them.

First, take a deep breath, then another. Next, identify the voice in your head. As already mentioned, you will notice familiar phrases like, 'You are not good enough'; 'You did a bad job there'; 'Don't make yourself look like an idiot again' or 'You shouldn't do that.' You might well have multiple Saboteurs, which is completely normal. If so, just pick one for now, and then come back to repeat the exercise to deal with the other saboteurs later.

If you are struggling to identify this voice, think of a time you experienced an emotion you didn't like, and listen to the voice behind it: What is it saying? It might focus on different areas of your life, such as fitness, work or public speaking. For now, detect the most prominent or loudest voice.

Take another deep breath. Now close your eyes and imagine what the Saboteur looks like. It can be hard to physically look it in the face but, by doing so, you diminish its hold on you. What do you see? What does it look like? Does it have a physical shape, or is it a feeling? What colour is it? Is it holding anything?

What else stands out?

Now create a profile for your Saboteur. On a blank piece of paper, draw a profile picture of what it looks like, and use colour to bring it to life.

Next, write down as many of the following details as you can:

Name:
Date of birth (i.e., when they were 'created' in your mind):
Tagline:
Interests:
Last active/checked in:
Status update:
Friends:
Groups:
Messages:
Events:
Motto for life:

Now whenever this voice pops up, you will have far more clarity about who is speaking and be able to stand apart from it and up to it.

+ *Notice who's driving the car*

Imagine that you are driving along a road with no one else around you. You can be in any vehicle you want and on any road you want. Take a moment and close your eyes to bring it to life. Notice where you are. What can you see? What colour is your car? Can you smell or hear anything? What does the road look like?

Now notice where your Saboteur is sitting.

Often, our Saboteurs jump into the driver's seat, grab the steering wheel and set the direction, choosing the roads they want to drive down. However, it is time for you to take control again and get back in the driving seat. *You* can choose your path. Decide now where you would like the Saboteur to go – perhaps in the backseat (in a seatbelt to lock it in!), in the glove box, in the boot or on the side of the road as you drive forward. It is irrelevant where it is, so long as you are in the front seat and driving.

Now take a moment to feel what it is like to be back in the driver's seat, choosing your path and your timings. Jot down how you feel.

In the future, when your anxiety rises, check in and see where your Saboteur is in the car. Perhaps it has sneaked back into the front seat, so you need to run through the steps in this exercise and make sure it returns to its designated area. Remember, you are the one in control of the car and the destination.

+ Be kind

Overall, be gentle with yourself. Saboteurs are crafty tricksters, so you are not going to get rid of yours all on day one. It is a work in progress, so bear with it.

To help this process along, write down your Saboteurs as they appear with their unwanted opinions and their *should* and *must* phrases. Then replace a *should* with a much kinder *could*. It feels softer and less forceful.

If you are still struggling to keep these voices down, I would also urge you to speak to a coach, counsellor or support network for further help.

My Experience

Oh, this voice (or even voices) can become so loud; they do not benefit me whatsoever and instead bring me down and make me feel small. I often need to remind myself to listen to my Best Self over my Saboteurs. I have found creating a profile of my Saboteur gives me the words to describe and understand it. The noisiest one in relation to my anxiety is Panicky Pete. He looks like a gibbering teenager with horrible skin, and he crops up at the most unhelpful moments.

When feeling anxious, I check in with the visual of the car. I see a red convertible cruising down a straight, open and clear road with the sun shining down. Sometimes Panicky Pete can be driving in the front, so I put myself back there, with my Best Self as my wing woman, and chuck Panicky Pete in the backseat where I can keep an eye on him. Sounds absurd, but this image ensures I am driving and don't get sucked into the chatter of my Saboteurs.

I have made many profiles over the years, and it is interesting how they shift and change over time. You may find the same to be true for you, too.

Go for It

Always shine a light on Saboteurs. By bringing them front of mind, their power diminishes. We all have them, but let's make sure our Best Self is in control and driving the car.

4.3 Create a Dialogue with Your Saboteurs

The world breaks everyone and afterwards many are strong at the broken places.
– Ernest Hemingway

Snapshot

As mentioned in the previous chapter, our Saboteurs are the little voices inside our heads that tell us we are not good enough and that there's no way we can do that. They are the part of us that holds us back and stops us from getting what we really want. They become louder and more active as soon as we stretch ourselves out of our comfort zone.

Saboteurs have a tendency to hang around out of sight, lurking in the shadows. Generation Panic has them in abundance, all disguised in different forms. They can claw at our backs, or their little mitts can cling on to our ankles and hold us on the spot. Their hold often feels heavy, constraining and painful. Sometimes a Saboteur will perch on a shoulder and whisper abuse, or spit right up close in our face, all red and angry. Other times, they can smoothly seduce us into believing something that's not true.

There is usually no problem in describing what they look like; they are well-known 'friends' even if we have not personified them yet. Their faces and overall appearance can come to us quickly, despite their ability to morph and develop over time.

Importance to GP'ers

Once we have visualised our Saboteurs, it is far easier to create a dialogue with them. By understanding their tone of voice, pitch and tempo, we can get an element of control back and jump into the driving seat again. Clarity helps us to dissect the way they *deliver* their message; Saboteurs often disguise their thoughts and voices so that they are appealing and seductive. By building an awareness of their tonality, we can spot them more easily.

For example, a Saboteur can murmur to us in an alluring voice, 'You can go on that walk today, because you can always do the big to-do list tomorrow. Go on, just wait one more day – no harm done.' When we're faced with a mountain of work, the dulcet tones succeed, and the Saboteur has the power. It is too easy to get sucked into it. However, by recognising that silky voice, an alarm bell goes off. We can take back control, and anxiety recedes.

Jump into Action

+ *Knock, knock. Who's there?*

Observe the voices that are talking to you and start to get curious about *who* is behind them. Perhaps think of a recent scenario where you were hard on yourself because of how you reacted to or felt about an experience. Who is speaking? Who is the Saboteur? Is it someone you know? A parent? A victim? A judge? A perfectionist? An overachiever? Recognise anyone?

Become aware of the chatter, but not involved in it. Simply notice. Every time a Saboteur 'strikes' is an opportunity to work with it. It is a chance to get to grips with your Saboteur, so don't fight it!

Once you have recognised the voice, then wrench, pull, cajole or otherwise bring it out from wherever it is, and put it in your hand right in front of you, in your line of sight. Then you can really look at it for all its worth. What does it look like? What is it wearing? How is it looking at you? (Revert to chapter 4.2, *Saboteurs*, if needed and carry out the profile task.) Remember to continue to breathe deeply as you regain the power from your Saboteur and begin to create a dialogue. Make sure you describe your observations on paper and/or draw them. Oftentimes, as soon as you expose your gremlins and can see them, they shrink and lose some of their scary nature and strength.

+ *Thanks, but no thanks*

Once your Saboteur is in your hand, strike up a conversation. Saboteurs are usually created from past experiences and are there to protect and warn you. Often, however, they are out of date and not useful anymore. You need to update them by telling them that you are okay and you do not need their help. But first understand why you have created your Saboteur. Ask it directly, 'What is your positive intention for me?' In other words, 'If there is a good reason you are here, what could that be?' Then, listen to its response.

Take a deep breath, and thank your Saboteur for letting you know. Speak out loud, calmly and authoritatively: 'Thank you for your time and concern, but you are not being helpful. I am all right, and you do not need to worry anymore for me.' Please adapt this into what you feel comfortable saying. Whatever the phrase, the intention remains the same – bring the Saboteur to the front, hold the Saboteur in your hand and observe why it is there before telling it *out loud* that its help is not needed.

In case that does not work, there are a couple of alternatives. You can start by laughing at it – if you can make fun of it, it seems to diminish and wither away. Or perhaps send it somewhere and in doing so give it a task that will keep it busy, such as sitting in a cupboard and playing with files, or getting locked in the kitchen for a few minutes. As mentioned in the last chapter, always question who is driving the car. If it isn't you, then get yourself back into the driving seat.

+ Say my name

Finally, give your Saboteur a name, something you can easily call it. And tell people you trust about your Saboteur(s). This will allow you to talk about it – 'Argh, Moaning Myrtle was in full force today,' or 'The Judge hated that meeting,' or 'I struggled with pressing "send" on the email as Perfect Paul wouldn't shut up.' Make it light, fun and easy to talk about. Encourage your friends to tell you about theirs.

Your Saboteur might well comment and pass judgement on this exercise; in fact, odds are on he/she/it will criticise it! Bear this in mind, knowing that Saboteurs get louder the more they know that you are gaining control. You don't want to fight your gremlin and get into a tussle. Instead, merely try to notice it and move on.

My Experience

I found some of the exercises here insightful. One of my regular Saboteurs, which hangs around my shoulders, is a black, spikey, sludgy, dark ball (a cross between a sea cucumber and a sea urchin). When I create a dialogue with it, it goes from this scary, repulsive mass that makes me uncomfortable even to look at it, to a softer, more approachable object. More often than not, through talking directly to it, I realise that it is terrified and is just trying to protect me.

Another Saboteur of mine is a very old stern judge-type figure with black gowns (think Professor McGonagall from *Harry Potter*), who passes judgement on everything I do as either right or wrong. Her positive intention is to make sure I push myself and do things to the best of my ability; this is clearly useful some of the time. However, there is also a cost to heeding her advice; it can hold me back and make me judge my own experiences as well as interactions with others. By creating a dialogue with her, I can understand her motivations, and her message becomes less intimidating.

Go for It

Remember that *you* are in charge of your life, so take up the reins again. The Saboteurs are usually created with good intentions to help you, but they are just a little outdated. So listen to them, reconnect with your own true voice and take back control by making your own decisions.

4.4 Non-Judgement

The higher we soar the smaller we appear to those who cannot fly.
– Nietzsche

Snapshot

We are our own worst critics. We are often too harsh on ourselves and judge our actions to the *nth* degree. For almost every decision we make, our afterthought is to run through what happened and analyse it – what could we have done differently? How could it have been improved? What did they think of us? What reaction did we want to have? How did we want to feel afterwards? What was frustrating about it? Where did it go badly? It goes on and on and on.

By continuously judging and evaluating what is happening around us and to us, we fuel our Saboteurs' chatter. When we critique ourselves, we trigger an undesirable spiral. The negative talk that runs through our head influences our general outlook, casting a dark cloud above us. As a result, experiences are seen as black and white, right or wrong. This can lead us to become angry, sad, annoyed and disheartened – all of which fuels our anxiety.

We can also project this negative thinking on to those around us, as we are quick to judge and comment on others' lives and potential shortfalls. Ironically, we can take pleasure from being judgemental toward them – i.e., we criticise someone else so that we feel better about ourselves. More often than not, what we project on to other people can be seen as a reflection of how we truly see ourselves.

We then brush over and generalise our thoughts by saying, 'It's just the way things are,' and 'Some things never change,' but we have a choice. We can choose how we *want* to react to our experiences and also whether we judge others.

As a first step, let's show a little more compassion by being kinder and gentler to not only ourselves but also those around us.

Importance to GP'ers

When judging others, it is as though a negative weight pushes down on our body. It can feel very heavy when we sit from a judgemental perspective. On the flip side, when standing in a place of non-judgement, we feel lighter, gentler and much happier. If we think of it this way, it is a no-brainer which perspective is best.

Being non-judgemental allows us to observe the world without offering damaging thoughts and opinions that belittle ourselves and others. We should be able to watch things pass in front of us rather than getting bogged down in the detail and feeling a sense of injustice. It only adds to our anxiety.

Jump into Action

+ *Keep calm & watch yourself*

Get curious about when you are judgemental and how you feel when your body jumps to a reaction. Is it tense? Does something leap in your tummy? Does your throat constrict? Just notice what happens, watch it from a distance as an observer and don't offer any level of judgement.

Building awareness of when you pass judgement – either on others or yourself – is far easier said than done, so jot down any moments that you feel judgemental. Is there a pattern? Are there any times that have surprised you? When you look back on the day, were there any other moments you didn't notice at the time but in retrospect are good examples?

Being able to pause and catch yourself in the moment can be challenging. Remind yourself that awareness is the first step.

+ *Make yourself numero uno*

Now let's try and be non-judgemental of ourselves. Start by putting yourself first and viewing yourself as number one, even if it is just for an hour. In that hour, believe that everything you do is right, that you are doing the best you can and there is little you could do to improve what's going on. Try to stop the critical voice and replace it with a far more understanding one that is on *your* side.

Notice what happens and see if anything surprises you. Now try to extend the time, perhaps by lengthening the power hour to ninety minutes.

+ *Create an ally*

Create a tangible vision of something that can represent being non-judgemental. It could be a creature, object or person. It can help to picture the opposite of your Saboteur.

Give it a physical figure. What does it look like? Is it hot or cold? How does it smell? Is it carrying anything? What is its name? What does it represent – perhaps kindness, calmness, compassion, sympathy or acceptance, to name a few? It could be all these things and more if you like. Use the same template for this ally as you did for creating your Saboteur's profile.

At any time in the future when you feel the negative judging voice rise up and start to get vocal, whether in relation to yourself or those around you, call upon your ally and let it take the reins. Take your ally around with you and feel the change in your body as you transition from anxiety and hurt to greater acceptance. Question how it affects your physiology. Does it impact your breath? What can you feel?

+ *Float on by*

Focus on your thoughts and emotions, but don't judge them. Imagine that they are an object floating by – a little boat, a cloud, a duck – whatever it is, try hard not to judge it. You could even have your ally sitting next to you to give you a boost!

Remind yourself that you can choose to focus on your breathing and let things pass by. You can decide where you want to focus your attention. Watch your object continue to float past you, and breathe in and out, 7-7-7.

My Experience

Although this concept seems simple, I have found it a crucial part of my toolkit. I have a very judgemental side that immediately interprets experiences as right or wrong (remember the judge like Professor McGonagall). Something rises in my chest, and I'm unable to swallow the lump in my throat. My Saboteurs jump to the forefront of my mind and start to chatter away. In these moments, I connect with a wise old monk. I have an image of this man who sits on a mountaintop and has no judgement. He is able to see the positives, and he is a wonderful ally. He brings a lot of wisdom and compassion, which is invaluable and calming in these situations.

Letting things float past me is a technique that I still struggle to remember, but I instantly benefit from it, as I'm sure you will too.

Go for It

Live by Walt Whitman's words – 'Be curious, not judgemental.'

5. Slow It Down

Slow and steady wins the race.
– 'The Hare & the Tortoise', *Aesop's Fables*

5.1 Meditation & Mindfulness
5.2 The Power of Silence
5.3 Digital Detox
5.4 Find Your Creative Flow

5.1 Meditation & Mindfulness

There is more to life than increasing its speed.
– Mahatma Gandhi

Snapshot
Meditation and mindfulness both give us the opportunity to press the pause button on our busy lives. Researchers in the

study 'Even a Single Mindfulness Meditation Session Can Reduce Anxiety' published in *Experimental Biology 2018* have found that you can reduce anxiety and 'derive psychological and physiological benefits' with even a single session of mindfulness meditation.

The aim of these practices is to live presently and consciously, in the here and now, which leads to us feeling less anxious. Both involve being aware of what is around us or what we are feeling in a moment, but not criticising it, just noticing. For example, when something stressful happens, such as not getting our point across clearly and succinctly in a meeting, we can just notice what has happened and let it go. By using these methods to focus on observing without judging, we can feel a deeper sense of calm.

Both of them, particularly meditation, bring about clarity. Through these mediums we are able to view what is going on as an observer, from a distance. Putting space between us, and what is happening *to* us, can offer freedom, as we can differentiate our thoughts from reality. As a result, we do not need to analyse our feelings and get bogged down in our emotions.

Deep breathing (7-7-7, from chapter 1.2) is also an important component of both practices, as it greatly benefits the anxious soul.

Importance to GP'ers

We often get caught up in our past and our future, where our thoughts and inner dialogue are riddled with doubt, fear, anxiety and stress. Instead, meditation and mindfulness encourage us to live in our present.

Meditation and mindfulness have been proven to reduce stress and anxiety. By practising these, we can better handle pressure in our lives. Both give us little windows in the day to slow down, be peaceful and appreciate the small things. These pockets of calm have a reflective quality that is needed amidst the hustle and bustle of our everyday lives. By creating the space to take time for us, we feel empowered and re-energised.

GP'ers live fast lives as good 'doers', i.e., able to get stuff done and plough efficiently through an ever-expanding to-do list. However, there are two distinct ways of operating: the doing and the being. Both have different benefits, and both in their own right need to honoured.

Meditation and mindfulness are all about the being – slowing things down and becoming mindful of where we are in *this very moment*. These practices give us the opportunity to simply be. In doing so, we will be far more present, rather than letting the past dominate our thoughts, or worries of the future overtake our today. Instead, we can keep thoughts as just that – thoughts – and therefore make better decisions.

For some people, it can be difficult when feeling anxious to sit still and focus the mind. So go easy on yourself. If this does not work for you, then try something else. If it does work, then great! Keep going. Either way, remember to find the best solutions for *you*. A quote from the film *Layer Cake* sums it up pretty well: 'Meditation is concentrating the front mind on a mundane task so that the rest of the mind can find peace.'

Jump into Action

+ *Find your sweet spot*

The most important thing with practising these techniques is to work out what suits you. Mindfulness and meditation can seem intimidating, so instead try calling it breathing – we can all do that. There are so many routes that you can go down here – using an app like Headspace, slowing down in a moment, colouring in, listening to guided meditations (I recommend Tara Brach's), immersing yourself in nature, lying on your back, practising deep breathing, reading a topical book – the list goes on and on. Try a variety of things and see what works for you. You can also get ideas by talking to those around you who are interested in this field.

+ *Find the time*

More often than not, when you feel anxious you will find reasons not to fit meditation and mindfulness into your day. Despite feeling this, it is important you find the time. Create moments for you to stop doing and start being.

On the other hand, when you feel stronger, you might neglect your meditation and mindfulness. This is actually when you need to solidify your learning and make sure it becomes a habit, so stick with it!

Diarise recurring calendar invites for the coming weeks and honour the time. A great place to begin is to devote ten minutes of your day to this, even just for some relaxing deep breaths. For most people, the best times are first thing in the morning or last thing in the day, when our heads are most clear. At these times, we are usually at home, so it is often quieter and more relaxing. Again, play around to see what works for you. Remember, you have to build in the time – it will not magically crop up into your day. So you must find the time and protect it in your daily schedule. Go on, block out some time right now.

If you are struggling to stick to your schedule, ask a friend, partner or family member to hold you accountable.

+ *Start small*

We feel fully alive when we notice the little things rather than just rushing through life with everything seeming to spin past us in a blur. So get curious about the small aspects of your daily life, such as drinking a cup of tea, having a shower, opening your emails or observing things like a flower, how you place each foot in front of the other, pavement cracks or just your breath. What do you notice as you focus on the detail? Be in touch with your senses. What can you smell? What can you hear? What can you taste, see, feel, etc.? There is no right answer. Just break it down and make it simple, as the mind has a tendency to overcomplicate.

+ *Notice what anxiety is to you*

Anxiety manifests itself in different ways in different people. Be aware of how *you* feel in an uneasy situation and what works best to calm you down and bring you back to centre. Journal or write down what you feel and what has the largest impact on reducing your anxiety.

Then do some research. Resources such as books, websites and podcasts can take you deeper on this subject and let you delve into each sphere of meditation and mindfulness in more detail. Explore further if it interests you, and notice what resonates.

My Experience

The most important thing for me with meditation and mindfulness is to find my sweet spot. When I was going through a particularly anxious time of life, several people recommended meditation and mindfulness apps. I tried them all and struggled with most of them, as I did not find them that effective. As I am a natural 'doer', asking me to slow down when everything felt like it was on fast-forward was too much of a stretch. I couldn't calm my body or brain down enough to even engage in the process.

So I took the pressure off myself and instead created a space and time that was quiet and reflective. There is no right way to do this. For me, the benefits of using an app are that it holds me to time rather than allowing me to impatiently cut the session short, which is often the case! Basically, I try to bypass the sabotaging thoughts that tell me I am doing it wrong and get out of my head, reminding myself that I don't have to find nirvana through a deep meditation. For me, meditation is an area that I must continue to work on.

Go for It

Remember, we are human beings, not human doings. We do not need to rush from one task to the next. Being fast does not always lead to more success and happiness; instead, it often leads to burnout. So, create the time through mindfulness and meditation to slow down and take a moment for you.

5.2 The Power of Silence

In the midst of movement and chaos, keep stillness inside of you.
– Deepak Chopra

Snapshot

Experiencing silence can be powerful. Even the act of sitting in solitude offers a release from our busy daily schedules. Sadly, our culture measures how successful we are by how busy we are. Our own self-worth is measured by our productivity and ever-lengthening to-do lists. We charge through our lives like raging bulls focused on material success. However, this mindset is in itself exhausting, and it's a sure-fire way to burnout.

As mentioned, many people in today's world are 'doers', meaning we fill our time doing things, when in fact, we need a balance of 'being' too. It is just like the yin and the yang; we need equal measures of both to live our life fully and to be fulfilled.

Often we will experience silence when we are on our own, which allows us to have a space where we can reflect peacefully and honour the 'being' side. The busyness of our day-to-day schedules can feel like a cacophony that is deafening and overwhelming. By retreating to a place of quietness, we can reconnect with ourselves and truly listen to what is going on inside us; we can feel calm amidst a loud world. A great visual to remember is sitting in the eye of the storm.

Importance to GP'ers

When we don't speak and just listen, psychologists and other health professionals have found that we heighten our awareness. We are able to notice what's going on around us rather than letting life pass us by. We can therefore gain a deeper sense of mental clarity and simplicity.

As mentioned in the last chapter, silence can also ensure that we are present in this very moment, that we aren't describing (and getting bogged down in) something that has already happened or might happen in the future. Speech is a medium that allows us to put words around our fears of the past or future. Therefore, silence is the antidote to ensure that we become present right now.

Finally, by being silent, we are able to listen to our inner voices – our Saboteurs and our Best Selves. At times they are not helpful, but we can still learn from them. The external voices can be deafening and distract us from what is truly going on. By pausing and being silent, we can connect with what is occurring internally. Our inner voices want to be heard, so by taking a breath and being at one with the silence, we can reconnect and listen.

Jump into Action

+ *Be kind to yourself*

Be aware that you live in a busy, noisy world. That makes silence difficult to be with, and our natural instinct is to fill it. We are scared, and the loudness of past experiences or the worry about upcoming events overwhelms us. So, start small and be gentle with yourself. You are working a new muscle, but it will be worth the hard work. As Lao Tzu said, 'Silence is a great source of strength.' Be safe in the knowledge that silence can be incredibly rewarding and empowering.

+ *Lean into the silence*

Find a comfortable position. Now take a deep breath, right to the corners and depths of your body where you feel tension. On the exhale, breathe out that tension. When you are ready, close your eyes and just be with the silence. Notice what comes up for you; all reactions and responses are completely normal and justified. Try to repeat this at least daily.

During this exercise, be sure that there is nothing in front of you and no distractions of any sort. Clear the deck, so to say, of any diversions – sound, visual, etc. – so that you enter into your silence from a clutter-free space.

If you want to challenge yourself even further, look in a mirror when being silent. Hold direct eye contact and notice what happens. Our reflection can often give us insight into what we are feeling. Do not forget that our bodies speak, as mentioned in chapter 1.4, so listen to what is being said.

My Experience

In the past I was not very good at silence. I usually sought out people for conversation. In the company of others, particularly new people, I felt the need to fill the silence and often babbled away with nervous, irrelevant chatter. Over the years I have tried to home in on my silence and become more comfortable with both others' and mine.

In doing so, I have started to realise how noisy the world we live in is. I find it can be quite calming to take myself to a quiet place – my current favourite is in the park by a stream. Although my natural urge is to invite ten people to go with me, I challenge myself to go on my own and be comfortable with the silence – no podcast, no music, no chatter. Nothing. I often go dragging my feet, but I find it relaxing and calming once I have done it.

Go for It

GP'ers will benefit from a bit more silence in our lives. As you work on becoming more silent, remind yourself of the following proverb: 'Speech is silver, silence is golden.'

5.3 Digital Detox

It's all about finding the calm in the chaos.
– Donna Karan

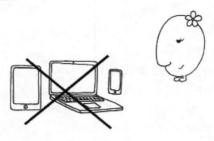

Snapshot

According to research published in a 2018 *Telegraph* article, 'A Decade of Smartphones', on average, a smartphone user will check their device up to nine times an hour … terrifying!

Our phones and social media make us feel as though we are a part of something, connected, in touch with others. The truth is we are addicts looking to find a distraction and escape from our everyday reality. That is why 24/7, we are hooked up online. We yearn for attention and validation from other people and try to feel 'boosted' by their profiles, when the reality is that we feel disconnected and crappy about our own lives. We link our value and self-worth to how many likes we get on social media, and as the likes increase, we feel increasingly special.

GP'ers are glued to electronics, and much of our life depends on them.

As soon as the morning alarm goes off, most GP'ers will reach for their phones out of habit, often without any thought or real need to pick them up. We then scroll through social media, trying to check for updates on how many likes we have or who has responded to our shares and pictures. The first thing that we look at every day is a tiny lit-up screen. How depressing!

Even the simple task of leaving the house is linked to our phones. For example, we might look up the best route to travel, get in touch with people we are meeting as well as Google the best place to meet, check the weather, book a cab and check the time. Then we might quickly scroll through Facebook or Instagram – and that is all before we have even stepped outside our front door.

Then at work, we are hounded by emails in an ever-growing inbox that are difficult to wrestle back to a manageable number. And so the hamster wheel continues to turn … and all the while, we are checking in on our phones, even taking them with us to the loo. Finally, before we close our eyes, most of us will revert back to our mobiles – a last check before we fall asleep.

As our anxiety levels rise, we feel increasingly dependent on our phones, yet our dependency on our devices leaves us feeling more anxious. Our phones help justify our lives, and we look for our self-worth to be validated out there in the world of social media.

Opinium has carried out research on the topic and found that nearly seven million people feel depressed when they see their friends' lives on social media. The party we weren't invited to, the picture we were not in … it can spiral quite quickly to make us feel unworthy. Likewise, the pressure to be happy, grinning madly and looking perfect at all times, is fuelled by social media. This kind of burden is not needed in our lives today. We already have enough things to worry about.

We need to stop, and stop now! It is sad that at a wedding, party or other event, people rarely experience the moment. Instead, we are all hidden behind a phone trying to get the perfect shot. And this happens so much whilst out and about – for example, when seeing the ideal sunset, we feel we need to take a picture of it rather than just watch it and be in the moment.

So, a digital detox is crucial. A digital detox is a period of time when you refrain from using any electronic devices, most notably your mobile phone, but also laptops, TV, tablets, etc.

Importance to GP'ers

We need to have deeper and better conversations with people around us and actually connect with them. Social media does not truly create a connection – it encourages us to hide behind a profile and try to project our 'happy selves'. We need to be aware that our desire to be liked and accepted will not be fixed through social media.

A digital detox allows us to choose how much time we spend on our phones, and therefore, it lets us take back control and reduce our anxiety levels.

Jump into Action

+ *Be real*

If you are honest with yourself, how many times do you think you pick up your phone each day? How long do you spend on it once you do pick it up? Do you get lost down the rabbit hole of social media? Do you take it to the loo with you? Do you slip it under your pillow?

Jot down or use an app to record every time you even reach for your phone. You might be surprised at how often you pick it up without even registering you are doing so.

+ *Step away from the phone!*

Put your phone down. Yup, that's right, *down*! It is that simple. You choose to take the power back into your hands.

To help, write down the benefits of having a digital detox. Ask yourself, 'What would this provide me with?' and 'What can I gain from a detox?' If anything comes out of this brainstorm that stands out, pop it on a sticky note and put it somewhere to remind you.

+ *Get on with it!*

Decide how long or at what times you wish to take a breather from your electronic devices. For example, it might be that you put on an out of office for the morning and only check your emails for half an hour in the afternoon. Or perhaps you buy yourself an alarm clock so that you do not even need to take your phone into your bedroom. Make it fun – pop a sign on your bedroom door that the room is a Digital-Free Zone, or something of that ilk.

Now tell some close friends or family about it to get their opinions. Who knows, they might well have tips about how best to combat any withdrawal symptoms. Or perhaps you might find someone else who wishes to detox with you. From there, you can turn it into a game – the first one to look at their phone has to do a forfeit.

And stick with it. Yes, it can feel really hard and as though you are coming off a drug (which in some senses, you are). Try to think of another time when you have overcome an addiction, perhaps giving up chocolate or doing dry January, for example. Think of what lessons you can take from that previous experience and apply here. Remember that there is always light at the end of the tunnel.

After you have done it for a couple of days, jot down what you have learnt. Take note of any reactions or surprise results that have cropped up, and remember to keep reviewing these notes.

+ Explore alternatives to occupy your time

One of the easiest times to jump on to our phones is when we are bored or feeling uncomfortable, such as when we are waiting for someone or travelling. Come up with some ideas that can keep you occupied in this time, anything from twiddling your thumbs to thinking about your dream holiday to going through your times tables. Perhaps brainstorm around that business idea you have secretly wanted to do, or think about a new hobby that you could try out. So whilst you are waiting in line for your drink at the coffee shop, you can put your time to much better use.

My Experience

I astound myself with the amount of times I pick up my phone without thought and mindlessly flick through. I have deleted all the social media apps off my phone, so I really have to think when accessing my accounts by typing the URLs into a search bar. I often place sticky notes on my phone with reminders like, 'Really?!' or 'Think About It!'

Like me, you may find it hardest to digital detox in the bedroom. I find it too comforting to have my phone on me and scroll through if I wake up in the night. This never leads to anything positive, but it is addictive and so easy to mindlessly do. I have tried buying an alarm clock and leaving all devices outside the bedroom, but I sometimes slip back into it. Like me, you will probably find that it is always a work in progress.

I also try to consciously decrease the amount of screen time I have on holiday; it is nice to switch off and have a break. Although it feels hard at the time, I rarely regret it, and I realise that the world really does not stop if I unplug for a week.

Go for It

Write a reminder and stick it on your phone, such as 'Are you sure you want to pick me up?' Remember that your phone is doing you far more harm than good. A digital detox will benefit any GP'er by decreasing our stress and anxiety.

5.4 Find Your Creative Flow

I don't know where I'm going from here, but I promise it won't be boring.
– David Bowie

Snapshot

Creativity makes us feel more alive and is a wonderful way to reduce our anxiety. Creativity can stem from a whole range of sources, and it leaves us feeling fulfilled and happy. Finding creative activities such as art, writing or dance can also help us to interpret our anxiety in a form that is unintimidating and free-flowing. Creativity can take many forms, depending on our individual personalities, interests and goals. Whichever route we take is right as long as it benefits us.

Generation Panic'ers often find that their creativity is stifled as they strive to fit in and follow the trends. GP'ers work in fast-paced, pressurised roles that have little to no room for creativity. Instead, we feel as though we are caught on a hamster wheel that keeps spinning, faster and faster, with no way of getting off.

On top of this, when we're anxious, it can feel as though our creative juices have evaporated. Our brains are void of all imagination and inspiration. Instead, we want to be in a state of flow, as Mihaly Csikszentmihalyi describes it in his TED Talk. This is when our mind is free and thoughts simply flow. Imagine a river meandering through the countryside. If we are 'in flow', there are no bridges, dams, built-up debris or other obstacles in the river; the water can run seamlessly. Its current builds momentum so that the water gets to its destination far quicker without any blockages. So the trick is to find the activities that offer this flow to us – tasks we become completely immersed in and that let us feel fully engaged.

Importance to GP'ers

Bringing creativity back into our day-to-day lives helps fulfil us, particularly as the creative method can be both enlightening and liberating. For GP'ers, creativity can help alleviate stress and take our minds off our rising anxiety. By permitting our imagination and inspired thoughts to flow, we can increase our confidence levels.

When GP'ers are not operating 'in flow', anxiety or even boredom kicks in, and we begin to feel the pressure rising. It can be hardest to achieve this seamless approach at work, particularly as many high achievers are doing jobs they dislike, jobs that don't use our natural creativity.

In contrast, when we are 'in flow', our concentration is focused. The mind is able to home in on a specific task, and we are not distracted by any interruptions. We are fully engaged. We are fully immersed. Aside from the obvious benefits of feeling more confident and happy, we will be doing activities we genuinely enjoy.

Jump into Action

+ *Play, play, play*

First, check in with yourself. Think about what type of mediums you already like working with, such as art, music, dance or writing. Then think about doing the following exercises for each one, or something similar if your activity doesn't appear in this list.

Art – Get a blank piece of paper and draw whatever comes to mind. Everything is right here. There is no wrong colour, shape or style. Leave your perfectionism at the door and see what comes out.

Music – Pick a song and see what impact it has on you. Dance however you want to when listening to this particular song. Pay attention to the rhythm and beat and the reaction it stirs within you. Just get curious.

Writing – Write for five full minutes about whatever comes into your mind. Many people refer to this as 'morning pages' and do it each day when they wake up.

You can implement any of these activities daily and see whether they impact your anxiety levels. If you are struggling to get started, pick a topic in your life that is frustrating for you and represent it through any of these mediums. The topic can be anything from feeling directionless to working towards a promotion to going on a date.

+ *Back to basics*
Dream up all the things you already do that make you feel calm, happy, peaceful and relaxed.

Then add other activities that you are interested in trying. The list is endless, and no idea is a bad idea. Don't rule something out just because it doesn't appear to be in keeping with what you would normally do. For example, listening to classical music may not be a regular pastime of yours, but try it out. Push your comfort zone, and know that if it doesn't work, there is no need to pursue it. The bottom line is to get creative and contemplate all areas of possible interest.

A few ideas to contemplate:

- Painting
- Running
- Meditating
- Playing an instrument
- Cooking

- Hiking
- Sewing
- Praying
- Biking
- Gardening
- Baking
- Drawing
- Dot-to-dot
- Listening to music
- Yoga
- Designing
- Reading
- Dancing
- Colouring in
- Walking

+ *Shoot for the long term*

Pick just a couple of activities that have caught your interest and try them out. Have fun! Write down any thoughts on each activity, how you felt, what you noticed and whether you want to do it again. Most importantly, did you feel 'in flow' with any of it? If you really liked some aspects but could tweak it to make it better (e.g., painting was good, but it could have been more fun outdoors), then try it out.

From here, incorporate whichever activities you liked into your daily schedule and build habits around them. For example, each morning draw for at least fifteen minutes to give you time in a state of flow. It will make you happier and help you realise that often it is the small things that count, as mentioned in the meditation and mindfulness chapter.

+ *Be messy!*

Play around, be messy and have fun! Bring back some childish exploration. The most important thing here is to remember to enjoy your activity. Stay curious about your creativity. It should be a fun and light process, so leave your perfectionist instincts at the door.

+ *Gain little victories*
Do not beat yourself up if you are not in a constant state of flow. In today's world, let's be realistic. Look to achieve the small wins. They are feasible and will let you more quickly achieve a state of flow in the short term. Over the long term, you can build on them and lengthen your times of flow.

My Experience

You may have noticed that this chapter is linked to mindfulness. In my pursuit of creative flow, most activities I've done make me feel very calm, relaxed and present. A particular relaxer for me is cooking, which helps me unwind after a stressful day. Likewise, I love being childlike, getting messy and having fun with dot-to-dot, colouring in and painting. I cannot emphasise enough how bad the paintings are, but I have such a peaceful time doing it that it is worth it (and no one ever has to see them!).

I also enjoy non-taxing exercise, such as walking and biking, which brings about a sense of calm and is a good time to think. The rhythm of it gives my mind space to breathe. I have always loved reading as well and find that it helps me escape; I can get transported to a different world that gives me a break from my reality.

Sometimes I get frustrated that I do not have a consistent flow with my activities. However, when in flow, I know it ... I feel a wave of peace wash over my body, and the chatter in my mind stills. Even ten minutes of this precious time is worth striving for, as it helps diminish my anxiety. I love reaching this state, and I can access it more regularly and easily now.

Go for It

Play around and get messy with these activities to find your flow and reduce your anxiety. Bring your inner child to the table and enjoy.

6. Recognising Success

Everything will be all right in the end, and if it is not all right, then it is not the end.
– John Lennon

6.1 Experience = Knowledge = Power
6.2 Peak Experience
6.3 Yes Person
6.4 Wheel of Life
6.5 Celebrate

6.1 Experience = Knowledge = Power

I have failed over and over again in my life. And that is why I succeed.
– Michael Jordan

Snapshot

Past experiences offer us wonderful insights and nuggets of learning; we can take invaluable lessons from what we have already gone through. Having conquered tough times and come out the other side reassures us that we can get through anything coming our way. In surviving past difficulties and analysing them, we can improve our mindset, gain wisdom and approach upcoming situations we might be nervous about with more confidence and the knowledge that we will get through it.

For example, if you are anxious about a big meeting coming up, rack your brain to find examples of similar occurrences, perhaps when you were nervous at a meeting but overcame it and had a successful meeting. It is encouraging to know that we have been brave before and therefore can do it again. This knowledge offers a welcome respite from our anxiety, particularly when we're faced with stressful situations.

Tracking what we have learnt from previous experiences can be a reminder that we are good enough. It can be comforting to remember this when doubt starts to creep in and all sense of rationality seems to fall out of the window.

Importance to GP'ers

When we are faced with challenging moments, it can (without seeming melodramatic) feel as though the world is about to end. Life feels heavy, and we can quickly lose perspective. Reconnecting with previous successes makes everything seem a little lighter and easier.

As GP'ers, we are often more emotionally resilient than we give ourselves credit for. We have surpassed many hurdles that we don't validate as being 'big enough' to acknowledge. However, it is certain that we have been through hardships and come out the other side, so let us use this knowledge to our advantage.

Jump into Action

+ *Go back*

Look at times in the past when you have gotten through difficult experiences and made it through to the other side. Jot down all ideas that come to mind, whether big moments or small wins – the more, the merrier! This will give you a range of experiences to call on when faced with challenging moments. Write everything down in one place so that you can easily refer to them when needed.

Now go through each one and breathe in that experience – relive it. Take what you learnt from that moment and apply it to where it is needed right now. Note what attributes helped you to advance. What makes you able to label them successful? What are the key characteristics you showed? What resources did you use?

+ *Mighty mantra*

Come up with a sentence that you can repeat when needed to reassure yourself. For example, 'Remember, I won the pitch in May, and came across as confident and articulate when asked challenging questions,' or 'I enjoyed that drink and had a good evening,' or 'I stayed calm when I was running late.' Tailor it to work for you, but try to fill the sentence with positive and uplifting language. Be optimistic – it will resonate with you more.

My Experience

This concept of acknowledging previous successes has played a huge role in helping me overcome anxiety-filled situations. When I was initially going through all my panic attacks, I literally thought that my world was going to end. I have never felt so low, lost and utterly helpless. On reflection, however, I have learnt so much about myself, and, at the risk of sounding clichéd, I have no doubt that it has made me a better person.

Taking smaller examples, I have had many meetings and interactions that have not gone well, anything from me losing all train of thought to needing to leave the meeting. I take whatever has happened that I am displeased with and try to learn from it, thinking about what I would change or how I could do better next time. Of course there is always room for improvement. But if I dwell solely on all the things that didn't go right and where

I messed up, then I will be unable to see anything positive. Instead, I have to change my mindset and look for the upside, even if nothing is immediately obvious.

It never fails to amaze me how much strength I can take from the mere knowledge that I have got through things in the past. So, for example, if today I feel particularly nervous before a meeting, I remind myself of much harder meetings that I have overcome – even excelled at – and it immediately calms me down. I have written down a collection of past experiences and 'wins' that I can use when I need it, particularly when my mind goes blank and I don't feel like I have ever done anything well.

Go for It

Give yourself credit for getting this far. With all you have already been through, you can get through the next hurdle for sure. Baby steps, but forward …

6.2 Peak Experience

Don't think limits.
– Usain Bolt

Snapshot

A 'peak experience' is euphoric. It is a time when we have felt fully in control and happy, a moment in which life feels particularly rewarding and we feel truly alive. A peak experience happens when our values are being upheld, when what is important to us is being honoured. Values can encompass anything we believe in, and they are central to the way we live our lives, such as freedom, love, friendship, adventure and travel. When our values are respected, it gives us a sense of calm.

Psychologist Abraham Maslow believed that everyone is capable of having a peak experience. He described these types of experiences as 'moments of highest happiness and fulfilment'.

A peak experience is not easy to come across, and we cannot set them up or plan for them. However, at different points in our lives, we have been in moments that felt true, honest, free and alive, and these can be counted as peak experiences. In these moments everything seems perfect, as though things have fallen into their rightful place.

Importance to GP'ers

GP'ers can start to access such an experience when we have momentarily forgotten about feeling anxious. Instead, we have been able to step into our true power and feel alive. We can freeze-frame that moment in our mind's eye and create a memory where everything from the colours to the shapes, smells and light is pretty much perfect; they come together to help create that peak experience.

We can then carry around this memory with all the associated emotions and feelings and use it to access a happier time at anxious points in our lives. By taking the time to connect with the mental photograph of our peak experience, we can immediately improve our mood.

Jump into Action

+ *Find the sweet spot*

First, take a deep breath and get comfortable. Now think back to a moment in your life where things felt good and easy. Just go with a time that pops into your head when you felt empowered and content and were living life to the fullest. Think of an occasion when things seemed to be going your way – all was as it should be.

Now bring that memory of your peak experience alive – so alive you can almost touch it. Notice where you are. Become aware of what the weather feels like on your face. Notice how you are standing in that particular moment. Observe the sights, sounds and smells. Go into the detail of the peak experience.

Then, whilst recalling this moment, ask yourself:

- Why does that memory stand out for me?
- What is happening in my body?
- Who was I being in that moment?
- What about this moment makes me feel connected?
- What values are being upheld here?

+ *Anchor it*

And now anchor this emotional state by finding a way to remember your peak experience. It might be an object, a song, a smell, a taste or simply the action of pinching your thumb and forefinger together. Search for a trigger that you can call upon when you want to access the experience's emotions.

For example, if your peak experience is when you reached the top of a mountain on a walk, your reminder could be the coat you were wearing that day, the selfie you took on the top, a key ring with walking boots on it, a mountain air spray, a song you listened to on your iPod to encourage you to get to the top, or the taste of the gum you chewed as you walked. Think outside the box, consider all options and really try to get into the moment, and you will discover the best reminder for you.

And now carry this reminder around with you so that even if you forget to access your peak experience, the trigger will do it for you.

My Experience

I have had a couple of peak experiences; however, the most visual, prominent and empowering memory that often arises is the time when my husband and I motorcycled across the Himalayas. One moment was profound: we were riding on a dirt track over the mountains. What makes it sublime is that it honours many of my core values – adventure, freedom, connectedness, relationships, aliveness and exploration. I often return to this moment when I am struggling and find that it helps me take an extra breath to bring about calm. I sincerely hope you can find at least one peak experience that you can call upon.

Go for It

Let your peak experience be a wonderful reminder of feeling confident, strong and happy so the anxiety ebbs away.

6.3 Yes Person

We become what we think.
– Buddha

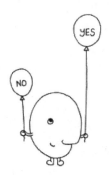

Snapshot

A 'Yes Person' is someone who says yes to all opportunities. In the film *Yes Man*, Jim Carrey's character agrees to everything that is asked of him, with no excuses. Although the principle is to be taken with a pinch of salt, it is still very powerful.

Anxiety often blocks us from doing things that would benefit us. We shy away from what we see as potentially dangerous situations (remember chapter 2.4 *Get Out of Your Comfort Zone*). We avoid difficult events and face challenges unwillingly. All the while, the Saboteur voice in our heads gets louder with 'no, no, no, no' or 'I can't do that.' At these moments, we need to be a Yes Person – essentially feel the fear and go for it anyway! Although anxiety often limits our action, at times, we need to just say yes, to push outside our comfort zone and go for it. We might surprise ourselves at what we learn and what we can get out of it.

There is a caveat: you must have a balance. Depending on each person and each situation, a Yes Person can be a people pleaser and as a result puts other people's needs in front of their own. In certain situations, giving priority to others can be dangerous and unfulfilling. Therefore, saying 'yes' to others can sometimes increase our stress and anxiety levels. If you are continually looking for approval in others and therefore put them first, you will get to burnout pretty quickly. Just be aware of this as you consider what it means for you to be a Yes Person.

Importance to GP'ers

Being a Yes Person can allow GP'ers to become more aware of the choices we make, and this level of consciousness can challenge us whilst simultaneously progressing us forward. Taking on this role can instil optimism and confidence as we push through our limitations. As a result, we can take on challenges and learn from our experiences. By saying yes to what we normally would not do, we can get out of a routine or a habit that is not benefitting us, and instead we can break the cycle.

For GP'ers, this might initially feel overwhelming. But in the long term, it will decrease your anxiety levels by exposing you to more experiences. Who knows what you might stumble across that has a profound impact on your life.

Jump into Action

+ *Yay or nay?*

Write down instances when you often say no. Now get curious: What is driving these decisions? If you take a bird's eye view of the list, what would you say is underlying a lot of your choices?

For example, if you say no to all social activities with friends because the fear of participating overcomes you. Perhaps it is a fear of being inadequate which actually underlies your decision.

Then ask yourself the following two questions:

- How is this benefitting you?
- What is this costing you?

+ *Stay strong*

Remember that you have a choice. In any case you can decide what is the best route forward, so consider saying yes when you can choose which path is going to benefit you most. If caught in a moment when someone asks for an answer, pause and say, 'Can I let you know?' Go away and ask yourself the two questions I just posed to you, and see where it leads you. Don't forget to check in with yourself and trust your gut (2.5).

When saying yes to experiences, believe it and say it with conviction and confidence. Others react well to those who know their direction, regardless of whether that direction is considered positive or negative. Stand in your power, and stand by your decision.

If in time it has not worked out, that is okay. Look at what hasn't worked, then learn from it, change it and move forward.

My Experience

For a whole year, I practised being a Yes Person, and it led me to some unpredictable and exciting places. It pushed me out of my comfort zone and exposed me to new things. The less positive side was not building in time for myself, so it came to a point where I needed to start saying no. I realised that I wasn't putting myself at the centre and desperately needed to make myself the number one priority. However, it is all about finding the right balance and being able to check in honestly with where you are at.

Go for It

All in all, connect with reality and see what is genuinely possible when you say yes. Push on to learn new things.

6.4 Wheel of Life

You can't focus on what's going wrong. There's always a way to turn things around.
– Joy, *Inside Out*

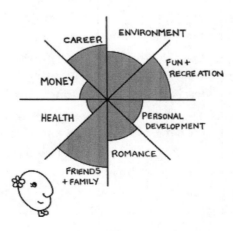

Snapshot

When we're struggling with anxiety, the Wheel of Life exercise helps us step back and take stock of where we are in any given moment. This is a successful and simple tool that I often use with my clients. It lets us break down our lives into distinct categories so we can look at the individual areas. At the same time, we can also gain a better snapshot of our lives as a whole. This tool can be a great way to get better clarity and bring more balance to our lives. It can also help us move forward with greater purpose, as it helps us set goals.

The easiest way to start is to picture your life in different subjects. It is helpful to draw a large circle on a piece of paper and divide it into slices like a pizza. Each slice represents an important aspect of life that can help you focus on that area (we'll get into specifics in a moment, but you can search online to get more details).

As you go through each slice, you will label and then score it from 0 (not achieved) to 10 (fully achieved). This will give you a good idea of where you stand in each category today.

Importance to GP'ers

It is important for GP'ers to pause and acknowledge where they are from time to time. We can then look at individual areas of our life as well as the whole by stepping back and looking at the bigger picture.

In our day-to-day lives, we often get bogged down in the categories that are not going well. We focus on the lower scores or the pizza slices that aren't fulfilled. This leaves us feeling downbeat and disheartened, only adding to our anxiety. However, when doing this exercise in its entirety, we can take off our blinkers and see what else is going on. We can begin to take back control and ensure that we are also focusing on positive aspects of our life rather than getting caught up in the negative parts. As a result, this exercise gives us the space to acknowledge and safeguard the parts of our life that are going well and even look to enhance them.

Jump into Action

+ *Draw the Wheel of Life*

Draw out a big circle on a large piece of paper. Now divide it into eight sections and label each section with a different category of life. The most common are:

- Environment
- Fun & recreation
- Personal development
- Romance
- Friends & family
- Health
- Money
- Career

However, you can play around with these categories with whatever works for you. Likewise, if you wanted to check in on one area of your life, you could break down the wheel into that topic. For example, if 'career' is the whole wheel, the slices could be broken down into relationship with manager; team building; personal development; progression routes; salary; job satisfaction and so on.

Now go through each category and rank it from 0 to 10, where 0 is completely dissatisfied and 10 is fully satisfied and content. This number does not represent where you *want* the category to be or where you *think* it should be, but instead where you are right now. It is best to fly through these scores so you get down your true gut feeling rather than overthinking it and being inaccurate. Once you have jotted down your scores, draw a bar at that level across the slice of pizza. So if the category of career is at a 6, ensure there is a line across this section of the circle at the level of

6. Once you have completed your scores and drawn across each slice at the score level, it should vaguely resemble a wheel.

+ *Look at the whole picture*
Step back and look at your wheel in its entirety. What do you notice? How is your wheel looking? Would it go around smoothly if it were an actual wheel, or would it be a bumpy ride with different scores and levels on each pizza slice? Is there one area that stands out to you? What else seems significant?

+ *Daydream*
Pick one area that you wish to focus on (you can repeat across all of them in due course if you want). Why have you picked it? What stands out about it? Then ask yourself what you would like the score to be (for example, is it a 3, but it would make you happy to get it to a 6). If it were the score you want it to be, what would that look like? What would be happening? What would be different? Who would you be? What would you be proud of? What else do you notice?

+ *Call to action*
Now think of three things you can do today to get you one step closer to achieving the score you want, and write them down. (If that is too hard, then consider what you can do this week.) So, for example, if you are a 3 for health and want it to be a 6, you could (1) cut out one caffeinated drink, (2) walk home rather than get on public transport and (3) go to sleep an hour earlier. They don't need to be big, but the aim is to get you moving forward *today*. Once you have these ideas written down, consider how you can take action on them, and take the first step now. You can do it!

My Experience
I find this exercise fast, fun and insightful. I respond to the

different segments based on a gut feeling, without thinking, so the true and immediate response usually comes out. Stepping back and looking at the wheel as a whole is also powerful because I am often surprised at how unequal it is. And then putting three things into action today feels fast paced and exciting – and it leaves no room for procrastination, which works really well for me.

I keep most of my wheels so that over time, I can check in. It is interesting to see how I have progressed and how what I am currently focusing on changes. I feel less anxious having an overview of where I am, as it makes me feel secure knowing that it is logged on paper. Perhaps you will relate. Although this is a simple task, it is a powerful one.

Go for It

Check in with your wheel regularly. Draw a few of them in your journal to take stock of where you are. This way, you can also remind yourself of previous scores, goals and actions. Get rolling!

6.5 Celebrate

The more you celebrate your life, the more there is in life to celebrate.
– Oprah Winfrey

Snapshot

Although we all think that we love celebrating – the joys of a wedding, a new job or a party – is the reality actually true in our everyday lives?

We rarely rejoice when we are doing well in our day-to-day lives, or when we have succeeded at something. It feels indulgent and even uncomfortable to pause and acknowledge something we have achieved. We are our own toughest critics and will continuously find ways to negatively analyse and pull apart what we have done. For example, if a presentation has gone well overall, rather than focusing on how successful the pitch was, we instead dwell on the moment that we lost our way and forgot what we were going to say.

In addition, we often strive so hard to reach our goals, such as getting a promotion, that when we get what we wanted, we barely pause for breath. Instead we are off working on the next goal. This mindset is a huge problem with fiercely driven people, as we are rarely satisfied with where we are. Imagine it in terms of climbing to a mountain peak. Highly ambitious people get to the top and are already looking for the path to the next highest mountaintop. Seldom do high achievers pause on top of the mountain, thrust their hands into the air and let out a loud 'Whoop!' of recognition for their accomplishment.

Importance to GP'ers

If we allow ourselves to do it properly, celebrating makes us feel awesome. When we pause to reflect on what we have done well, we can acknowledge the hard work that has gone into getting to that stage and give ourselves a pat on the back. We should respect this powerful moment of recognition. If we do not stop to celebrate, it will be hard to motivate ourselves in the future. How can we inspire ourselves if we are not rewarded for our hard work? We need to be proud of what we have achieved, and celebrating is the first step.

By celebrating, we can take a moment to recognise our strengths and what we are doing well, focusing on the 'good stuff' and boosting our morale. Likewise, in the act of celebrating, we can also ponder what we have learnt from a positive perspective. We can then improve or reproduce the process for future occasions.

Quite simply, celebrating success when it is justly deserved makes us feel good and empowered. It also inspires those around us. If they can see that you are able to pause and celebrate, they will feel encouraged that they too can do the same.

Jump into Action

+ *Go small or go home*

First, set small goals so that you have many chances to celebrate. Praising yourself should not be valid just when you have achieved a massive accomplishment. We can also celebrate ordinary achievements every day. Only if we take a break to applaud the small things will the taste of success be even sweeter.

So pick out some little goals now that you want to achieve, anything from going to that yoga class to replacing your caffeinated drink or meeting an old friend for a catch-up.

+ *Dream it, believe it, and achieve it*

After you have picked out a goal, write down the goal and what the outcome will feel and look like so that you have a point of reference. You would be surprised how in time your mind can play tricks on you, telling you to strive for the next goal without acknowledging this one. For example, if you say, 'I want to save £100 this month,' you might forget to celebrate that achievement once you get there. Or perhaps you might think to yourself after you save the money: 'This doesn't really justify a celebration; only if I hit £200 will I celebrate.'

If your goal is in writing, you are far more likely to remember it and uphold the promise to celebrate when you accomplish it – regardless of whether your feeling in that moment authorises doing so. The goal you set in the first place is likely a stretch anyway, so don't belittle it or come up with excuses when you achieve it to avoid celebrating. You would be surprised how easy it is to do so!

+ *Celebrate success*

Now think of *how* you would like to celebrate. It can be anything you want. Perhaps at the beginning you can go big and make it mega! For example, if you would like to celebrate that you signed on a new client this week, then have a dinner with your family and give a short speech about how you are proud of this accomplishment.

Do let others know that you need their help to celebrate your wins. It will be fun for them to support you and feel proud along with you in the celebrations. Celebrating has an infectious quality, so tell others and get them on board! Friends, family members, colleagues or partners can hold you accountable to celebrating the small things – anything from brushing your teeth twice a day, cooking a great supper for friends or smashing a work meeting. Get creative and think of ways you would like to applaud yourself by the end of the week. Then celebrate with a nice dinner, by picking up your favourite chocolate bar or by giving yourself an uninterrupted hour on a Saturday morning to spend as you please.

My Experience

In the past, as soon as I got a promotion or a bonus, or when something positive happened to me, I would think, 'Great … what next?' My reaction to go to the next goal would be so fast that I wouldn't give myself time to stop and celebrate. I had to cultivate the mindset by starting to celebrate even the smallest things.

I now set clear goals and ensure I do something to celebrate once I have hit them. I love eating, so it is often a dinner out or raising a glass. Honestly, even a chocolate bar has worked wonders! I cannot tell you how nice it feels to celebrate something properly. And my anxiety calms down, as I am not whizzing on to the next challenge and getting consumed with it. I urge you to pause and celebrate – you'll feel fantastic.

Go for It

Celebrating the mundane sounds simple, but it is harder to follow through with than you think. There is probably a voice in your head discouraging you to do it, saying something like, 'I don't need to buy a chocolate bar when I finish a work document that I am proud of; how silly!' However, there is no doubt that when you bite into the chocolate, or however you take a moment to appreciate that awesome piece of work, it will feel good. So have a go and don't forget to celebrate.

7. Change Your Perspective

Everything we see is perspective, not the truth.
– Unknown

7.1 Fresh Perspectives
7.2 Change of Scene
7.3 Right Frame of Mind
7.4 Our Qualities as Seen by Others
7.5 Works Well When … Even Better If … (WWW … EBI …)

7.1 Fresh Perspectives

Impossible is just an option.
– Paulo Coelho

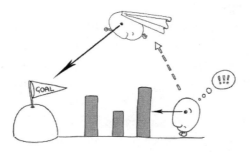

Snapshot

When feeling slightly on edge, it is easy to get bogged down in the moment, as panic sets in and our anxiety rises. At these times, even the smallest things can have a huge impact on us. It might well be that we have not achieved what we wanted to during that day at work, we have been late for a meeting or perhaps we have had an argument with a family member. It might be as simple as not feeling confident enough to go out. Anxiety becomes all-consuming, as though a fog descends over us and makes it hard to see a way forward. We get caught up in our minds and our emotions; the same negative, self-limiting thoughts go around and around our heads, and we begin to spiral out of control (as with the running track in 2.6, *You Are Not Alone*).

At these times, we desperately need a fresh perspective. As the proverb says, 'Instead of complaining that the rose bush is full of thorns, be happy the thorn bush has roses.' We need to find our roses. We need to shift the way we are looking at the situation to help get out of our rut. It can be hard to change our perspective, but it can be done. And once we have done it, we will feel infinitely better as we have more choice on how we want to respond and how we can best move forward.

We can gain a different perspective by looking at other people's qualities and adopting them. This is particularly helpful if we feel we do not possess a desired skill or life experience. For example, if we wanted more decisiveness, we could look at Winston Churchill and take on this perspective of his personality. Or in relation to communication, we might question: How would Oprah approach the situation? Or if we could bring a lighter, funnier frame of mind: What would Mickey Mouse do?

Fresh perspectives can also mean looking at our situation from a different angle or a different point in time. For example, how does the same topic look from the view of a helicopter, or five years in the future? It is amazing how much our perspective can shift by changing our frame of reference.

Importance to GP'ers

Finding a new way to view any problem can alleviate the associated pressure. By changing our perspective, we are reminded that we have choices and can decide on the direction we want to take. The fog begins to lift as we step away from our immediate situation and get a fresh perspective on it. We can begin to see clearly again and think rationally. Consequently, our anxiety starts to subside, and we take back control of our bodies and thoughts.

Jump into Action

+ *Change places*

Identify an obstacle that has held you back recently or is holding you back at this moment. Now physically change your perspective. Go outside! Get some fresh air and walk around, or find a peaceful spot to sit. Come rain or shine, go and do something different. Sitting there in your anxiety, spiralling further and further down, deeper and deeper, is not going to help. Even if you are really busy and do not feel as though you have time, find a little window, even if it is only five minutes. It will save you in the long run by helping you to be far more productive and alert, rather than sitting there becoming more and more panicked.

If you feel yourself getting stuck in a negative mindset and your anxiety is rising – for example, you might be working towards a deadline or have an upcoming meeting – it can be a struggle to step away. However, you will get more done if you look after yourself in this moment.

When physically changing your perspective, remember to breathe deep using 7-7-7. Do not hold your stomach in but really relax – let your tummy swell out, and inflate it with fresh air. Let the new air fill you, literally breathing in new life, and take it to the bottom of your gut.

+ *Imagine your BFF*

Imagine that you are talking to your best friend and they have come to you with the same problem you are having. The tables have turned, and now you are the one giving advice to yourself. Answer these questions out loud as if you were speaking to them:

- What advice would you give them?
- How would you speak to them? (Notice your tone, language and pitch – I guarantee it will be different from how you speak to yourself.)
- How do you view the situation?
- What do you know is true for them?
- What are they doing well?
- What would you reassure them of?

Switching roles often highlights that we are much kinder in our interactions with friends and give them far more leeway and support than we do to ourselves. It can help you to treat yourself in a nicer way too. So just imagine you are helping out your best friend and give the advice accordingly.

+ *Shake it up*
Try standing in the shoes of other people who can offer you some pearls of wisdom. Pick any of the following or anyone else who springs to mind that you think might have an interesting perspective:

- Your three-year-old self
- Your eighty-year-old self
- An actor/actress you admire
- A politician you respect
- A family member
- Your favourite singer
- A local serviceman or servicewoman (e.g., firefighter)

Now move to a new space on the floor and literally 'step into' this person. Then ask yourself out loud:

- How would they stand?
- What would they be saying?
- What would they be wearing?
- What would their voice sound like?
- What advice would they offer?
- What can I learn from this new perspective?

Now repeat, trying out other voices and see how they differ. Breathe deep and enjoy listening to this new advice. What do you want to implement?

+ *Run a film*

This is a great exercise when you feel overwhelmed. It gives you the chance to be a fly on the wall and look at the situation from a safe distance.

So pull up the situation and run a movie in your mind's eye. Then imagine you are twiddling with the remote and can change things to what you want. Put it in black and white, make it softer or louder, closer or further or pop it on pause – you have the power, you have control. Change the way you are seeing the situation to alter how you are reacting and coping. Refer to chapter 2.6, *You Are Not Alone*, for some more tips to help you get a fresh perspective.

+ *Go up high*

Imagine that you are in a helicopter, or that you are a bird soaring high above, and get some distance from your current situation. Notice what changes when you put space between you and what's going on. What does being up high give you? How does it shift your perspective? What can you see from up there? What else can you learn?

+ *Fast-forward*

Jump ahead five, ten or even fifty years from now. As your future self, what do you know to be true? What advice do you want to give to your current self? What does your older self wish you had known at this moment?

My Experience

Anxiety makes me feel as though I am trapped and glued to the spot. I can't think clearly, and all I can see is the anxiety. By changing my perspective and using these techniques, I become unstuck and can breathe again. In fact, I use the action points on rotation depending on whichever is going to suit me best in each moment. One minute I pretend I am a little toddler version of Agi, and the next minute I imagine I am a famous actress. My failsafe, which works a treat, is flying up high as a bird to get some distance and perspective on my situation.

I have to remind myself to quieten the Saboteur's voice saying it is a stupid game and I look like an idiot. Once I have bypassed these opinions and step into their bodies, into how they would think and act, it is enlightening. More often than not, my anxiety ebbs away.

Go for It

Have fun with this one. See your 'stuck' areas from a fresh perspective and realise you have choices on how you respond.

7.2 Change of Scene

You can do anything if you have enthusiasm.
– Henry Ford

Snapshot

It is important to get away every now and then in order to have a change of scene. We all need a break from our day-to-day lives. It is crucial that we get a little perspective, particularly if we begin to associate our anxiety with daily battles, such as leaving the house and travelling to work each day. By changing our physical environment, we can get some respite.

It is a real struggle to get off the hamster wheel. As the wheel gathers momentum, it goes so fast that it is hard to keep up, and we lose control. The faster it goes, the harder it is to gain clarity and see the situation for what it is. Eventually, it hinders us in heading where we want to go.

Changing our scene to escape our normal lives does not have to be expensive, time-consuming or difficult. We can easily find something to match our budget and time frames. Even just escaping to the park for an afternoon or a day trip offers huge relief. Be spontaneous – have a picnic or take a beautiful walk and immerse yourself in nature. The criteria is anywhere that gives you a fresh perspective and allows you to escape the bubble. Get creative with your time and money and push yourself to try new experiences or do things you have always dreamt of.

Importance to GP'ers

When we get caught up in the daily grind, our outlook becomes clouded and negative. It can be hard to motivate ourselves in the repetitive days that roll into each other; no day seems different from the last, and life just ticks on by.

By breaking the pattern of everyday life and broadening our horizons slightly, we can release some of the pressure. Anxiety will decrease as we begin to open our minds and escape. In doing so, we can expose ourselves to new environments that stimulate us in different ways and give us respite from our daily worries. As we internalise and digest new surroundings, we have more mental space and can gain greater clarity of mind. This new perspective will leave us feeling more positive and far more in control. Shake things up and change the norm.

Jump into Action

+ *Create clear boundaries*

It is important you know your boundaries, so first of all, look at your budget and decide if you want to go with anyone. You do not need to spend a lot of money or even any money, as there are many excursions to do for free, such as going for a walk in your local park, visiting a free museum or swimming in the sea. Just getting outside into nature can work wonders.

+ *Dream away*

Plan fully for what you would like to do at the place you have chosen. If you are staying for a longer time, you will need to consider what you want to get out of your time away. Consider setting targets so that you have clear and strong intentions for your escape – perhaps doing a digital detox by turning your phone off (5.3), thinking about your future and dreaming big (9.4), or finding your creative flow by painting daily (5.4).

Have a good think about things you have always been interested in, but perhaps felt too scared to pursue. Push yourself to do what you have been putting off, and challenge yourself, such as by taking a silent retreat or learning how to surf. Push the boundaries of your comfort zone (2.4), and get your thoughts in your journal.

+ *Deepen the learning*

It is important to reflect on the time that you have had away and get curious about what you have learnt. This does not need to be a time-consuming exercise or a chore; instead, make it fun. Use your imagination to reflect on what you are taking away from the experience. Maybe you could create a playlist that represents your time away, paint a picture that reflects the park or keep a journal.

If you write about the time, here are a few pointers:

- What did you love about the time away? Even if it was a complete disaster, find something, however small, to write about.
- What did you learn about yourself?
- What are you proud of?
- How could you make the next excursion even better?

+ *Plan round two*

Whilst you are riding the high of being away, use the momentum to book another trip or make other plans to break away from your everyday life. Even if it is a few months away, it is wonderful to have something to look forward to, especially if you write about your plans in your diary. If it wasn't a successful trip, even more reason to book the next getaway; learn from the past trip and create a better one next time. Book it and get it in the diary – *now*. And do not forget to come back to your notes and review them later to remind yourself of the impact the experiences had on you.

My Experience

I really value getting away from my everyday reality. By taking a break, I can gain some perspective on how things are going and begin to think clearly. Yes, trips often come with anxiety too (I'm not great in airports, or returning to reality), but most of the time it is totally worth it. Even walking in a local park is usually a wonderful release for me. The lead-up also gives me something to look forward to, and I never fail to get the next one in the diary!

Go for It

Get out of the bubble to get some distance from and perspective on life. Just give yourself a break – mentally and physically – and enjoy the time away.

7.3 Right Frame of Mind

The last of the human freedoms [is] to choose one's attitude in any given set of circumstances.
– Viktor Frankl

Snapshot

When anxiety grabs us unexpectedly and constricts our breathing, it is difficult not to get dragged down by it. It feels like a dark abyss of negativity that we are trapped in, and it keeps us paralyzed with fear. The Saboteurs get louder and louder, pulling us backwards and holding us hostage in a dark place. This can be damaging and limiting.

Our anxiety rises when we believe that everything is against us and nothing is going our way. Problems become catastrophic, and the stress of it all can lead us to recall negative things that have happened in the past and forget about the positives. One thought can impact our mood significantly – for better or for worse. This means that we can wake up each morning and feel defeated before we have even started the day. Our negative mindset can debilitate us, and our attitude restricts our potential.

Our frame of mind is critical because it determines how we move ahead with our daily lives. That concept is easier said than done, but we need to make a conscious effort to be happy. By cultivating a positive outlook, we can go and achieve what we truly want to, no limits. The right frame of mind will get us dreaming and thinking about what we can do in the future, but it has to be positive. That means we must stop complaining and cut out the negativity.

There is an old Cherokee story that perfectly sums it up. A grandfather tells his grandson about two wolves fighting inside him; one is greedy and angry, and the other is kind and generous. The grandson questions, 'Which wolf wins?' to which the grandfather replies, 'The one which I feed.'

So which wolf are you feeding?

Importance to GP'ers

By stepping into the right frame of mind, we can be confident knowing that our opportunities are endless. A positive outlook ensures that we are continuously growing towards what is important to us, and therefore we feel much happier. Instead of letting negative thoughts rule, we can look for the upside and put our worries into perspective.

A good way of adopting this mindset in our everyday lives is to ask ourselves, 'What is the 2 per cent of goodness that I can find here?' For example, if we are caught on a tube that is delayed, 2 per cent of goodness might be that we have the chance to pause, be present and breathe. Or if we have completely messed up an important pitch and didn't win it, the 2 per cent of goodness could be that we have learnt exactly how not to pitch and the steps we need to take to improve next time.

It is all about our frame of mind. Our reactions to situations and how we internalise them determines how we feel about them. If we choose a negative outlook – the wrong frame of mind – it dominates our thoughts and leaves us feeling miserable. However, if we step into the right frame of mind, we can create self-awareness, confidence and a positive attitude. This ensures we feel calmer and more in control, something that all GP'ers will benefit from.

Jump into Action

+ *Take a stand*

Decide that you *want* to have a positive frame of mind. You are a fully capable human being and have the choice at your fingertips. So make the decision and choose to have the right frame of mind. Positive outlook, here we come!

Think about what you can control and what you can't. Often you can control your reactions and your emotions, but you cannot control other people and their reactions and emotions. Knowing this means you can stop wasting time worrying about trying to control other people and instead the onus is on you to focus on controlling your own responses.

+ *Start every day on the right foot*

We are not happy all the time, particularly when dealing with the natural and regular highs and lows of life. However, it is important to take the time to work out what does make you happy. What does it consist of? Is there something that works every time? What are the benefits of being unhappy? Be realistic – some people are naturally more optimistic than others, so tailor these questions to what works for you.

Then, write down your answers. The list does not have to be long, and you can leave some space to add to it over time. Now put it where you can see it every morning, perhaps by the mirror or where you brush your teeth. This will allow you to start every day with the right frame of mind.

+ Look the part

An easy way to change your frame of mind is to dress to impress. This sends messages to our brain that we are taking pride in ourselves. Caring for our appearance also impacts how the world perceives us. You might be surprised how much this will affect your positivity. Test it out: Carry out your tasks for the day in a pair of tracksuit bottoms and an old T-shirt that is in need of a wash. The next day, wear something colourful, smart and well-tailored; it's not about money, it just needs to be clean, ironed and presentable. See how each outfit impacts your outlook. Positive dress = positive mind.

+ Chill out!

We can easily slip into a woe-is-me mindset. Catch yourself so you can jump out of it and replace it with a more positive mindset. Tell yourself: 'Lighten up, it's not all that bad.' This might not work for everybody, but there is some truth here, and it can act as a good reminder that things are not as bad as they seem. If this expression doesn't resonate with you, think of another way to communicate the underlying message.

+ Do a reality check

To help you build up your strength and put yourself in the best frame of mind, ask yourself:

- What is the worry?
- Is it helpful to have this worry?
- Is this worry true?
- What is the worst thing that could happen?

+ *Remember 2 per cent goodness*

In every situation, ask yourself, 'What is the 2 per cent of goodness that I can take from this situation?' Although it may seem all doom and gloom, there is always a silver lining to every situation, however small. You just need to find it. And be patient; it might not spring to mind immediately, but the knowledge that it is there is sometimes enough.

To help you recognise the good, create a character who embodies appreciation and gratitude. Is there someone who holds this mindset that you can aspire to? Or perhaps you can create a character from scratch who has all these traits. To help bring them to life, build a profile for them, as you did with your Saboteurs (chapter 4.2). In the future, you can call on this character when you need to find the 2 per cent of goodness.

My Experience

Like you, I have a *choice* about how I wish to approach and work through my anxiety. I can shift my frame of mind (although doing so is hard at times) and change the way I am handling it. Even how I get up in the morning and thinking happy thoughts from the outset can have a profound impact on my day. It is like a new muscle that needs to keep developing, as it is so easy to slip into negative thinking. I also find if I make the effort in the morning to get dressed, make the bed and start the day 'smart', then the odds are stacked in my favour to have a better day than if I rolled out of bed and wore some old, crumpled clothes, rushed out the door without making the bed and let the anxious thoughts run the show.

Aside from this, my go-to in many anxious situations is the 2 per cent of goodness. However hard things get, however difficult the day becomes, when I find that 2 per cent, the anxiety releases somewhat. I sincerely hope that you can begin to adopt this mindset of asking yourself where the 2 per cent of goodness is in *every* situation.

Go for It

You have choices, so feed the right wolf and step into the right frame of mind.

7.4 Our Qualities as Seen by Others

There's something you must remember ... you're braver than you believe, and stronger than you seem and smarter than you think.
– Christopher Robin in *Pooh's Grand Adventure: The Search for Christopher Robin*

Snapshot

When our confidence hits rock bottom, it is difficult to think positively and find anything that we do as right. All we seem to do is blunder from one mistake to another, fumbling through life and feeling useless. If someone asked us in such a moment what our strengths are, most of us would find it challenging to think of anything. And even if we did, finding the confidence to say it out loud is daunting.

It does not need to be this hard. Even if we do not see the positive characteristics in who we are, it is guaranteed that others around us do see our strengths, particularly those who know us well. We may think they are biased and therefore not take their views seriously, but it is worth listening to them, as some of what they say must be based on at least a smidgeon of truth. If they hold up a mirror for us with their words, we can begin to see a reflection that we might eventually believe in.

Importance to GP'ers

GP'ers need to boost their confidence, and what better way than to acknowledge our attributes? We can collect a list of our strengths and personality traits that represent how others value us. Knowing that we are viewed this way by those closest to us can have a positive and profound effect on our confidence. It might well illuminate something we have never considered about ourselves. It might be confirmation of an area we are proud of, or perhaps it could be something we have never given much thought to but that is clearly important to the other person when they think of us.

All in all, understanding our qualities from the perspective of others can lead to us feeling happier and overall more positive. It can create a sense of worth knowing what our friends, families or colleagues see, and truly value, in us.

Jump into Action

+ *Get in touch*

Choose a few people to contact about your qualities, ideally at least five to ten (the more, the merrier). Drop them an email or talk to them face-to-face, whichever appeals more to you. You can decide how open and honest you wish to be. However, I would advise you to be your most authentic self. Then say something like, 'I am really struggling with my confidence at the moment, so I wanted to get your help and hear about what you value in me.' Or perhaps even simpler: 'What strengths of mine do you admire?' Tailor it to whatever you feel most comfortable asking.

Don't worry if any of the answers reveal similar messages or the exact same message; if anything, a repetitive response should reassure you that the trait is a powerful and core strength of yours. Store all the responses in one easily accessible place – and that means *all*, even if they are repetitive or if you deem them silly. You could print them out and stick them in a book, or draw a representation of what they symbolise. On days when you are doubting yourself and not feeling strong enough to face the world, the responses can serve as a wonderful reminder of how people value you and how you contribute to the lives of those around you.

+ *Return the favour*

Take it one step further and respond to every reply you get by telling that person what you appreciate about them – even if they have not asked you to! Rarely do we speak to our closest loved ones and tell them what we love about each other. Perhaps jot down three things that you love and admire about them and send those replies in a note. You will be surprised at the impact you will have on people. Always look to return the favour and pass the good vibes on!

My Experience

When I was at my particularly panicky stage of life, I doubted my strengths and what I was good at. In the midst of a panic attack, I could not think of anything I could do well, and I did not feel good enough. I have therefore used this process of asking people what they value about me to build up my confidence. I have only asked those I am very close to, so my next challenge is to ask people in my wider network. What has surprised me about the responses I've received was how many characteristics I took for granted as 'just the way I do things' were seen by others as big strengths. Consequently, when seeing these qualities from their perspective, I appreciated the power of this exercise in improving my outlook and mood.

Go for It

Focus on your strengths, and try to bring them into your daily interactions with others. It will make you feel happier and will help you realise you can have a greater impact on those around you.

7.5 Works Well When ... Even Better If ... (WWW ... EBI ...)

Do not be embarrassed by your failures; learn from them and start again.
– Richard Branson

Snapshot

WWW ... EBI ... stands for 'Works Well When ... Even Better If ... '. This concept allows you to get curious about how you can improve any scenario rather than criticise it.

Look at a recent activity or experience that you are proud of; it should follow the 'WWW' part of the acronym (e.g., in a meeting at work, 'works well when ... I spoke up and delivered my point with clarity').

Then, see where you could improve or what you could do differently in future scenarios. Pop this under 'EBI' (e.g., 'even better if ... I stood with more conviction and held eye contact for longer').

By using this structure, we can gain further clarity and avoid mistakes. We can learn from our experiences, see where we can improve and recognise our strengths.

Importance to GP'ers

GP'ers often struggle to celebrate successes and be proud of little moments (6.5, *Celebrate*). We either move on quickly from achievements without giving ourselves credit, or we devalue them by thinking they are not big enough to merit reward. The format of WWW allows us to notice what we are proud of and where we have excelled without being too intimidating. It captures the essence of what we have done well.

The EBI part allows us to give ourselves constructive feedback. We can work out where we could improve next time and how this would alter our experience. In doing so, we will be constantly developing and applying our previous learning to upcoming scenarios.

By using this framework, we capture our experiences and check in with ourselves as to what has happened. And the process of writing it down is beneficial because it makes us more conscious of our decisions. Rarely do GP'ers create this pause for themselves, but it affirms what we naturally do well and also highlights a stretch for the next scenario.

Jump into Action

+ *Apply it*

Pick a topic that you wish to focus on – perhaps an ongoing conversation with your boss, a gym session or public speaking at work. You can keep it broad if you feel like that would be more suitable for where you are.

Sit down daily and look at what you have done in this particular area. You can even add it to your daily journal (*Gratitude Book*, 8.2). Follow the WWW … EBI … mantra and go into detail about your experience. Get curious and write down your thoughts into the framework – it can just be a gut reaction and be completed quickly. You can review these notes over time and see how the topic has changed or shifted focus.

My Experience

Although WWW … EBI … is a basic concept, I apply it to many parts of my life and love it. It speaks to my Judge Saboteur, who likes to comment and pass judgement on everything. This mantra satisfies her in a constructive and kind way. After every meeting or client session, I will ask myself 'WWW … EBI …' to get to the crux of things clearly and concisely. I can analyse myself and look deeply at my actions whilst offering constructive feedback. The more I use it, the more I rely on it! I hope that you get as much out of it as I do.

Go for It

It is so simple. Write 'WWW … EBI …' at the bottom of your diary or daily notes, and see how your anxiety diminishes with each improvement!

8. Appreciate the Small Things

For the great doesn't happen through impulse alone, and is a succession of little things that are brought together.
– Vincent van Gogh

8.1 Gratitude
8.2 Gratitude Book
8.3 Acts of Kindness
8.4 IAA (I Am Amazing) Notebook

8.1 Gratitude

Gratitude is the single most important ingredient to living a successful and fulfilled life.
– Jack Canfield

Snapshot

Gratitude is a concept that seems to have taken the world by storm! Many people today swear by its effects on their lives.

Gratitude is the quality of being thankful. It is a state of pure happiness in which we learn to appreciate the different parts of our lives for the good and the bad, and can pause in the moment to be grateful for them.

When it comes to gratitude, we need to remember to look at the small things. Often we hear people say they're grateful for the love of a person close to them, or grateful for the regular income they receive from their job. However, gratitude can apply to anything simple and seemingly minor – the wind on our face, a single flower standing tall, the light of a candle, a cup of tea in bed or a short walk. However small it may seem, it is still significant.

Robert A. Emmons, PhD, a global expert on gratitude, says that the practice of gratitude falls into three main camps – physical, psychological and emotional. The benefit of gratitude most notably leads us to becoming a healthier, happier and more optimistic human being, thus impacting not only our own lives but also the ones of those around us.

Our ability to be continuously aware and grateful is a skill that we can cultivate. Gratitude develops and deepens gradually, but we must remember to invest our time and energy into making it a conscious practice.

Importance to GP'ers

The practice of gratitude is powerful and gives us a wealth of positive emotions. For GP'ers, it teaches us to slow down, focus on little things and acknowledge the good in our lives. All of this helps to combat our anxiety and leaves us feeling calmer, as we see the joys in everyday occurrences.

We can use our senses to connect with what we are grateful for and most importantly appreciate what's simple, even something like the act of helping another person or enjoying the taste of that delicious meal. If we focus on finding these little moments, we will live in the present and in doing so improve our mood and feel more positive.

Gratitude can also block negative emotions and in effect build a 'gratitude wall' around us – a solid, high and protective barrier that ensures we are able to celebrate the present. The wall also shelters us from toxic reactions from others and the worries of the past or future.

It's true that embracing gratitude can be difficult. It challenges us to pause and find something we are grateful for when we feel as though the world is against us. It is also tough to slow down when life seems to move so quickly. However hard it might be, do try to go slow and look for the positives, as it offers us the chance to breathe and bring more calm into our everyday lives. When our anxiety levels begin to rise, this is a great place to have more peace and to get off the hamster wheel.

Jump into Action

+ *Go slow*

A good way to learn to slow down and find gratitude is to walk at your normal pace, then at half your speed. Halve it again. Halve it again. Halve it again. When you have slowed down as much as you can, challenge yourself to halve it again! What do you find you appreciate when you take your foot off the gas?

+ *It's the little things*

Become inquisitive about your day-to-day life and start to look for the small things as well as the big obvious ones. What are you grateful for?

Write down how you feel in your journal, noting this variety of small and big things. How does appreciating these impact you? Do you feel happier? Does your happiness change depending on the size of the subject, for example, a flower versus a person? What can you learn from this process?

+ *Pause right here, right now*

Notice when you become increasingly anxious and the fight-or-flight response kicks in (chapter 1.1). Your heartbeat rises, your mind goes blank, your palms start to sweat and your stomach begins to somersault. At that moment, take a deep breath or two using 7-7-7 and pause. Forget about what is upcoming or what has happened. Park your anxiety and worries to one side in your mind's eye. It is hard to do so, but remind yourself that they are just placed to the side, so you can go back to them whenever you want. However, use this free space to ask yourself: 'In this very moment, what am I grateful for?' However small it is, focus on it.

My Experience

When I halve, and halve, and halve again my walking pace, I am amazed at how my bouncing thoughts can transform to much calmer ones as I notice and appreciate new things. However, for me, the slowness when halved even again can feel really sluggish, and I begin to get impatient. In many ways, this exercise sums up my opinion of gratitude – it's sometimes insightful and powerful, and sometimes a bit slow and woo-woo for me. There are many proven benefits that show how great gratitude is, so it is an area that I am always looking to develop. Breathing and slowing things down is a good place for me to start, and when I get out of my head and try to be present, I am often pleased to be connected and experience the power of gratitude. Other methods speak to me more, but perhaps it will work well for you.

Go for It

Let deep thanks and appreciation rule the day, and in doing so, let it wash away your anxiety as you focus on what you are grateful for.

8.2 Gratitude Book

Wisely and slow. They stumble that run fast.
– William Shakespeare

Snapshot

Most people, at some stage of their lives, have kept a diary or journal to jot down their innermost thoughts. It can be difficult to make it a regular habit, as it seems like a long and arduous task. Just finding the time to write in it daily can feel like a big burden that we often procrastinate our way out of. We think it is not a quick process of jotting down our thoughts but instead a laboured exercise that requires time and effort. We feel we must get more in touch with our feelings rather than having a quick solution.

Author, entrepreneur and podcaster Tim Ferriss suggests a number of practices, particularly around gratitude, that we can add into our lives to ensure we have the most powerful start and finish to every day. Gratitude journaling is one of them. And the best part is that it is a quick process that does not take long, so we can check in every morning and evening – there really is no excuse.

First thing in the morning, we connect with ourselves, get present and give focus to the day. Then at the end of the day, we can take a moment to see how we have got on, look for improvements and set up for the following day.

If you are struggling with the title 'Gratitude Book', then call it something else. Don't let the terminology put you off. It can be anything you want: a journal, a daily check-in, morning pages, etc.

Importance to GP'ers

As mentioned in the last chapter, gratitude is proven to have a positive impact on many areas of our lives, from feeling less isolated to having more joy and pleasure. Practising gratitude really works and can significantly increase our happiness and decrease our anxiety.

It is important to sit down daily to check in with ourselves and our emotions. Create a new habit by doing this regularly, as consistency will help this become part of our daily routine. Reflecting on where we are at a particular moment in time, and being open about it, is a release. Likewise, jotting down what we want to achieve in our day gives us direction and focus.

An added benefit to GP'ers is that by keeping a book/journal/record, we can keep an eye out for key themes that help us better understand our anxiety. Who knows, it might throw up ways that we have handled our anxiety well and reveal a different coping resource that we have used. We can begin to take back control by noticing what is going on.

Jump into Action

+ *Take note*

Get a book that you can label as you want, perhaps 'Gratitude Book', 'Daily Brilliance' or 'Morning Thoughts'. Keep it in a place that will remind you to use it every single day (the most obvious place being next to your bed). You can also create a daily reminder that will prompt you to use it, perhaps an alarm on your phone or a sticky note on your shower. Look to create a new habit out of this. To help, find a time that works well for you daily, for example, having just showered and had breakfast, when you are fully awake and feeling ready for the day. This could be a good time to pause and jot down ideas.

It really does not need to take long. Try not to overthink the answers; just jot down your gut response. Overall, it should take a maximum of five minutes. If you are pushed for time, put your ideas in your phone, which you can update in your book later.

Remember: be honest. It is crucial that what you write down is truly in touch with where you are at that exact moment. No one needs to see the book (or even be aware that it exists), so keep it real.

+ *Morning!*
Each morning, write three things under each heading:

I am:

Achieve:

Grateful for:

For the 'I am' section, write down how you are feeling in that moment. For example, 'I am on edge' or 'I am frustrated' or 'I am calm' or 'I am happy.' Simplicity is key! Keep in mind that nothing you write is wrong, as long as it is true to where you are in that moment.

Under 'Achieve', note three things that you want to get out of the day. They can be small or big – just check in with yourself on how you are feeling in that moment. You could, for instance, jot down 'Achieve: carving out time to read' or 'Achieve: good meeting with my boss' or 'Achieve: feel less anxious when seeing my friends tonight'. Try to stretch yourself, but also be realistic (*Get Out of Your Comfort Zone*, 2.4).

Under 'Grateful for', write down three things that in that moment you are genuinely grateful for. Choose at least one thing that is small and simple, such as 'Grateful for the warm sun' or 'Grateful for the vivid colour in a flower'. Then revolve your remaining answers around other things you are grateful for, perhaps 'Grateful for a wonderful friend' or 'Grateful for an income' or 'Grateful for a roof over my head'.

+ *Evening*

At the end of each day, check in with yourself to deepen your learning and look at ways you can improve. Fill out the following titles:

Achieved/Proud:

Improvement:

Tomorrow:

Under 'Achieved/Proud', reflect on what you have accomplished that day. Did you reach a goal or complete a task that has been bugging you for a while? Perhaps something new happened that you are proud of, such as having a great conversation with your boss, or managing to get present and notice something small. It doesn't have to be big – even a tiny accomplishment works.

'Improvement' is not a place for judging or criticising yourself. It allows you to get curious as to what you could do better in a future situation. For example, 'Improvement: Take a twenty-minute walk around the block for my lunch break,' or 'Improvement: Gain awareness that I am in a fragile place today, so avoid alcohol with friends.' Remember WWW ... EBI ... from chapter 7.5. You could change this title to use the WWW ... EBI ... format or add a line to incorporate it into your evening routine.

The 'Tomorrow' section is used to get you focused on the day ahead, as it can improve productivity. You wake up the next morning with clarity and direction from the outset; no chance for faffing around! So write down three things that you want to achieve tomorrow.

This exercise is much simpler than it may seem, so give it a go. As soon as you get the hang of it, it should be a fun and enlightening process. Each day should take only ten minutes total: checking in in the morning and reviewing at night. If it is taking longer, ask why. What is blocking you from completing this task?

+ Check back in
Keep all your records, and from time to time, look back on them. You will find it interesting, and at times amusing, to see where you were a few days, weeks, months or years ago. Begin to look for patterns and see where you might need a boost, where you can avoid something or perhaps what you can celebrate! Have fun!

My Experience
I heard about a Gratitude Book from the brilliant Tim Ferriss. I practise his morning and evening ritual every day to get connected, clear and confident about the day ahead in the morning, and to reflect, celebrate and look ahead each evening. This process calms me, as it makes me take the time to be honest and accept what is going on. I look forward to checking in daily; it is the perfect way to start and end the day – and then look ahead to the next morning. Because it takes so little time, there is no reason why I cannot complete it. As a result, it is one of the practices that I carry on through life – unlike a New Year's resolution that is only kept for a month! Like me, you may consider it cathartic to only keep your journals for a few months and then throw them away.

Go for It
Journaling is the most powerful way to bookend your day, to help you feel peaceful and be more focused and productive.

8.3 Acts of Kindness

No act of kindness, however small, is ever wasted.
– Aesop

Snapshot

We regularly get wrapped up in the daily stresses of our own lives, rarely giving thought to what is going on to people outside *our* version of reality. When we get bogged down in our anxiety, it can be hard to see the good in the world. Instead, we are fully consumed by our own struggles.

An act of kindness is simply being kind to those around us in a spontaneous moment. Our actions can brighten up someone's day, and most importantly, put someone else first. Sure, we might feel great from it, but that is not the primary motivating factor.

An act of kindness can also mean appreciating those around us, and actually telling them of their importance. A small comment can go a long way, yet it is shocking how often we forget to compliment others or tell them how much they mean to us. Saying something kind like, 'You are generous,' 'You are courageous,' 'You are brave' or 'You are intelligent' is a powerful mood-shifter. As humans, we crave being seen, and this type of appreciation will make the receiver feel as though they truly have been seen.

It is funny that people in their final stages of life often say that all they want is a hug or a cup of tea with loved ones. Kindness radiates through these simple gestures. So, why wait until someone is ill, or not bother just because they are a loved one? Go and be kind to everyone, and see how they react.

Importance to GP'ers

It is important to carry out acts of kindness, as even the smallest deeds can have a profound impact on others. By giving the most important gift of our precious time to someone else, we are reminded of the power and kindness of humanity. These are the moments that stay with us for a long time.

GP'ers particularly can get so wrapped up in ourselves – our own insecurities, our own worries and our own anxieties. Sometimes we need to see beyond ourselves, to open our eyes to other people's needs and take our mind off our own problems. We must forget about us for just one moment and invest in another person. When we pour all our attention into them and put them first, it frees us from getting bogged down in our personal worries and gets us out of our head. Furthermore, by being kind and helping others, we feel as though we are a part of something bigger, and our existence has more meaning.

Jump into Action

+ *Get going!*

Plan or be open to acts of kindness in any given moment. Open your eyes and ears to what is going on around you, and think about how you can help. Use your imagination and start challenging yourself.

Here are some ideas:

- Help a child or an elderly person on to the bus.
- Take a cup of tea to a homeless person.
- Pick up a dropped item on the floor in a supermarket and pop it back on to the shelf.
- Compliment a colleague on what they are wearing.
- Smile at a random person on your commute to work.
- Help someone in need on the Tube (perhaps offer to carry a suitcase, help a parent with their pram or offer your seat

to someone).

- Pick up rubbish on the street and put it into the bin.

If you are ever stuck for inspiration, search online for 'ideas for acts of kindness', and you will have suggestions galore! Lack of ideas is not an excuse.

My Experience

A moment of kindness that has stuck with me for years was when a fellow commuter I didn't know went out of his way to help me get home during a thunderstorm. On coming out of the Tube, I was caught with nothing for the downpour, and he put me under his brolly and took me on my way. I will never forget it.

Acts of kindness can be so small yet so profound. They should become second nature so that we automatically lend a helping hand to those around us. During my most anxious times, I was consumed with myself and my own miseries. I wish that someone had taken me out of those situations and shown me that there were other people around me who could benefit from these small acts. Now, I try to make acts of kindness a part of my day; you never know the impact you might have on someone else.

Go for It

The Dalai Lama once said, 'Just as ripples spread out when a single pebble is dropped into water, the actions of individuals can have far-reaching effects.' Although we might only do something small, it can have the most beautiful impact on both the surface of the water and in the depths. The ripples build and in time become waves. May you begin to have 'far-reaching effects' by the random acts of kindness that you carry out. There is no time like the present to start.

8.4 IAA (I Am Amazing) Notebook

I'm a slow walker but I never walk back.
– Abraham Lincoln

Snapshot

An 'I Am Amazing', or IAA, notebook gives us a chance to write down everything that we are proud of, or have excelled at, in one place. As we discussed in 6.5, *Celebrate,* we pass through our days, weeks and years without ever really taking note of what we have done well. This exercise lets us regularly acknowledge all the good things that have happened in our lives in a little notebook, which we can label 'IAA'.

A good starting place is to add three things each week that we are proud of. It can be anything from 'went to the gym when I said I would', 'worked with a new client', 'stood up for myself in a discussion', 'supported a family member', 'enjoyed [list a particular moment] with no or low levels of anxiety', 'felt stillness when I sat in the park' or perhaps 'had a lovely evening with a close friend'. It might also be seemingly insignificant things, such as, 'washed my hair today', 'helped someone with their shopping', 'was very present when walking' or 'appreciated my breakfast'. Realistically, big things such as getting a promotion, becoming engaged or receiving a salary increase happen rarely. So whilst we wait for the great moments, we must take pride in the small things.

For IAA, we need to be fully prepared to toot our own horn. More importantly, we need to be able to *recognise* when we have done a good job. We are naturally self-critical and judgemental of what we have done thanks to our Saboteurs (4.2). So push past the voices that say, 'You haven't done anything of note,' and find accomplishments to write down, however small or silly they might appear. Although it can be uncomfortable to admit what we have done well or are good at in general, it can be invaluable to our self-esteem as we have our successes in one accessible place.

This is a tough exercise to act on, but it is worth it in the end – I promise.

Importance to GP'ers

The IAA book reminds us that we are able to succeed more often than we give ourselves credit for. We can also influence our mindset, despite often feeling as though we are out of control.

Most importantly, our notes give us the best chance of remembering little wins so that we do not forget them and can relive them in the future. These moments add up, so the booklet can be used when we have a down day and nothing seems to be going our way. When we don't feel on our A game, we can go through the IAA book to boost our confidence and make our anxiety subside. All GP'ers will benefit from an IAA book to help us feel more self-assured and powerful. The effect can be quite immediate – we instantly feel the positivity that travels through our body when we remember a moment.

Jump into Action

+ *Carry a small pad*

Buy a small transportable notebook so that you can easily carry it around with you. It can live in your bag so it is close to you at all times. If you are feeling a little wobbly or are having a bad day, you can reach for the booklet and give yourself a much-needed boost. Get into the habit of reverting back to it to help manage your anxiety.

+ *Remember that you are awesome!*
Get brainstorming, and write in your IAA notebook as often as you can. Just get some experiences down (both big and small), and from there build your ideas. Don't overthink the content – be all-encompassing from the start! You can always change something if needed. And remember to be kind to yourself, as you are your own harshest critic.

My Experience

My IAA notebook is a Key Ring Memo Block from Muji, a staple that I often carry around with me. When I am feeling particularly anxious or having a bad day, I read through the book and am immediately uplifted. The instantaneous positive impact is often a huge relief; it replaces anxiety with confidence that I can do it and will get through it. Writing in it often is key; it's amazing the amount of times I read through it and think, 'Oh, yeah, I forgot about that!'

Go for It

Keep an IAA on you so you can easily add to it and remind yourself that you really are awesome, even when you don't feel like it.

9. Onwards & Upwards

There are better things ahead than any we leave behind.
– C.S. Lewis

9.1 Your Life in Its Entirety

Hell on earth would be meeting the person you could've been.
– Unknown

Snapshot

A eulogy is read at a funeral to all the family and friends of the deceased. Essentially it is a celebration of the life of a person who has passed away, a snapshot of what they achieved and how they lived their life. It usually focuses on their positive achievements and celebrates them for what they have given to others. It usually gets to the heart of who that individual was, what they stood for and their impact on others.

We each have a story to tell, and we are (or should be) the lead character in the plot, rather than someone else running our lives. So play out the story by writing your own eulogy. Write it as a script or the acts of a play – past, present and future. By writing our story, we will have more courage to live it out to the full. Often when reflecting back on our lives, we home in on the choices that we have made – and life really comes down to which path we have chosen to take. The key concept here is that we have a *choice*: the ability to choose our path, choose our reactions and choose our attitude. We can change any of it if we want to.

Importance to GP'ers

Writing our own eulogy lets us take the time to pause and reflect on our lives – both what we have done but also what we hope to achieve in the future. The principles and structure that go into creating a eulogy benefit us by offering a different perspective. Most importantly, it is a compelling way to get a new angle on our anxiety, as it takes us out of an anxious time and looks at the whole picture (7.1, *Fresh Perspectives*).

Moreover, the benefit of hindsight can be useful. We can use this exercise to look back for advice and tips and therefore see a clearer way forward. This exercise challenges us to ask provoking questions about what we want to be remembered for and who we really want to be. By connecting with these thoughts, we're reminded to live each day fully and with purpose to build the life we want. Do not wait until your deathbed to think, 'If only I had done this' or 'I wish I had done that.' Carpe diem, let's write our own story instead, starting now.

Death in itself can teach us so much and offers meaning to our lives. So make sure that you are living out today with no regrets.

Jump into Action

+ *Write an empowering eulogy*

Sit down and take a moment to breathe and compose yourself. Know that although you are doing a task that might seem morbid (and quite frankly, weird), there can be a lot to learn here.

Now imagine that you are in an out-of-body experience where you can objectively look at yourself from a distance. Take a deep breath and imagine that you are writing your eulogy from the outside, as though you are an external commentator. An older version of you has died at the end of your life, and it is now time for you to reflect on all they have been through and achieved.

Imagine that the eulogy you are writing will be read out loud, so start with a welcome, or perhaps a poem or a quote, such as, 'The trouble is you think you have time' (Jack Kornfield, *Buddha's Little Instruction Book*). Then just go for it, and see where it takes you. It can be sad, thoughtful, funny and/or serious depending on what tone you want to strike. See the following advice for some ideas on what you can include.

Remember, this does not have to be a perfect manuscript that is actually going to be read at your funeral. And this is a tough task, so be kind to yourself.

+ *Go back to the start*

It's best to start at the beginning. How did you come into this world? What was your childhood like? How did you get on at school? Even if you didn't enjoy school, mention it in a thoughtful and kind way. If you are stuck for inspiration on your life so far, flick through old photos and videos. You could even consider asking others for their advice on what they feel the highlights of your life have been so far.

+ *Future focus*

When looking to the future, get creative. What do you really want to do? How do you wish to be remembered? You have full artistic control to write whatever you like. Think out of the box and put yourself in the best light by including positive experiences and achievements to come: perhaps going on a trip, doing a career you love, living abroad, starting a family, etc.

+ *Takeaways*

On completion, reflect what you can take away. What you have learnt? Has anything surprised you about what you have written? Are you happy with the legacy you are leaving? Do you like the decisions you have made on the direction of your life? Don't judge the overall quality of writing, but instead get curious about the actual content. Question the importance of these moments being remembered and mentioned.

+ *Add-ons*

Here are additional powerful questions to ask yourself and answer on paper:

- What motto would I want inscribed on my gravestone?
- What do I truly want in life?
- What is most important for me?
- Was there a turning point in my life where things radically changed?
- How can I get from where I am right now to where I want to be?
- If I had one lesson to share, what would it be?
- What do I truly value?
- If I had sixty seconds to explain what life is about for me, what would I say?
- What quote best sums up my attitude toward life?

+ *One month left*

If you had only one month left to live, how would you use the time? What would you change, and what would you keep the same? Jot down your thoughts to offer insight.

My Experience

I have written my own eulogy and found the process powerful. I discovered how I wanted to live my life and what I wanted to be remembered for. The picture was clear and came readily to me, which surprised me. I think my gut knew deep down what I wanted to acknowledge and be known for. Interestingly, the smaller things, the relationships and the values I uphold stood out rather than the anxiety or the achievements I thought I wanted. Noticeably, my panic attacks and anxiety were such a small part in the bigger scheme of things.

The 'add-ons' I often answer in quick-fire question mode and treat as a bit of fun. My gut reaction speaks, and my head stays out of it. Again, it is a confidence boost knowing that my fundamental values are being a kind, grounded and good person rather than how much money I've made, or what promotions I have received. Likewise, the 'one month left to live' is a regular daydream of mine; I love thinking about how I would focus my time and what is important to me. Anxiety and the worries of everyday life seem to evaporate as I instead consider what I value most: family, friendships, laughter, sports, games, travel, reading, crosswords ... My last month would be filled with these rather than worries about things I cannot control. This process helps me to get back into the driving seat.

Go for It

Let your eulogy give you awareness of where you are today, as well as clarity on your future direction. Happy writing!

9.2 Future Collage

The world of the future is in our making. Tomorrow is now.
– Eleanor Roosevelt

Snapshot

A collage of our future offers clarity as to where we are headed, and bringing together images and words can reveal what we want. Having this visual reminder will decrease our stress levels and ensure we keep on track.

A future collage is essentially a collection of pictures that inspire us, a visual representation of what we would like to have. They can represent anything from the money we want to make to our ideal body, being an excellent public speaker, the travel we want to do, the title we want at work, having our friends and family over for dinner, a paint pot that represents our creative side, that TED Talk we have been planning, the book we want to write, the family we want to start. Dream big; the bigger the better. It is a fun activity to do over a relaxing afternoon and even provides a chance to find your creative flow (5.4).

The best is yet to come, so the clearer we get on what we want in the future, the more likely it is to come true. Clarity and momentum towards the destination will help to reduce our current levels of anxiety by focusing us and eliminating ambiguity.

Importance to GP'ers

A collage acts as a trigger to help remind us of our purpose and our future. Also, because ideas often build over time, having a visual point of reference can keep us advancing. It is an insightful tool to help us move forward with confidence. By getting our future ambitions on paper, we can then question how we want to change our behaviours now, and which direction we should head in. In short, our goals become clearer and simpler.

There is no point having amazing ideas that sit idle in our heads. Collages let us bring them out so they are glaring at us, which can prompt us to move forward and prevent us from getting complacent and lazy. GP'ers are often ambitious, but when we are overwhelmed with anxiety, we can get caught in 'safe' routines. Therefore, because a collage reminds us of our overarching goals, it can help us get unstuck and moving toward what we want again.

Jump into Action

+ *Remember, anything goes*

Buy a couple of magazines. Broaden your range and get different ones, such as a sports magazine, a showbiz one, a weekend newspaper and perhaps one from your area of interest – home renovation, cooking, finance, etc.

Then, flip through and cut out anything of interest. Have no filter at this point; just take out all pictures, words or articles that inspire you in some way. If something resonates in your body, then trust your gut and use it (2.5). Even if it feels unachievable or represents an area that you wish to grow in, take it out.

Once you have all your clippings, sort through them and see what stands out. Arrange them on a piece of paper and then start sticking them down. Remember to leave some space in case you want to add anything in the coming weeks as new thoughts spring to mind.

To get creative, make the board attractive with different fonts, colours and images. If you do not like the style of a clipping you pulled from a magazine, then take the time to find the right picture or draw something yourself. There are a wealth of resources, so add in what you feel is most suitable to ensure the mood board speaks to you.

+ *Get them up!*
Now stick your collages up as visual reminders, somewhere you can see them regularly, such as on the fridge, by the mirror where you get ready or in the bathroom. When you see them, don't just flit past them and think that you know what is on them. Take the time to focus in on particular areas and truly think about what it means, how you can embody it and what it gives to you.

My Experience

I find this light-hearted activity fun, relaxing and insightful. Even writing this now makes me want to go out, buy some magazines and create a new one. What I want is always changing and evolving, so I like to do it regularly. Because my collages are often close by, I can quickly refer to them to remind me of what I want. I am very visual, so this helps me know what I want more than writing, talking or feeling can. If you aren't visual, think about how you could do this in a different way that's more suitable, like through a collection of songs, food, etc. In doing this task, my anxiety ebbs away as I think about the bigger picture and what I want to achieve. I am held to a higher purpose and get out of the everyday niggles.

Go for It

Use your collage to get you excited and forward-thinking. The collage is a reminder that you can achieve whatever you want in the future, as long as you put your mind to it now.

9.3 Elevator Pitch

Don't be afraid to give up the good to go for the great.
– John D. Rockefeller

Snapshot

An elevator pitch is the practice of taking thirty seconds to sell who we are to someone in a lift, hopefully as it rises through the building to the penthouse! The assumption is that we are riding the lift with someone who is very important and could impact our career.

In contrast to the original definition of an elevator pitch, it does not need to revolve around a business objective or company's mission statement. The intention here is to write an elevator pitch about *you*. What do you stand for? What are your priorities? What messages do you need to mention to ensure maximum impact?

In short, how do you sum yourself up? You can start by getting your story straight.

Importance to GP'ers

If we are not clear on our own elevator pitch, it will be difficult to progress forward with conviction and confidence. GP'ers can benefit from having clarity about who we are and what we stand for. Knowledge of our own story (and how it comes across) will help propel ourselves forward with crystal-clear purpose. In doing so, we can greatly reduce our anxiety levels and build our confidence.

Let's begin by telling ourselves the right messages, not negative ones, and notice the knock-on effect this has on our levels of positivity, clarity and confidence. With a strong personal elevator pitch, the path in front of us – which can at times seem winding, dangerous and challenging – becomes clearer. We will then have the confidence to start putting one foot in front of the other, even if we cannot see beyond the next bend.

Jump into Action

+ *Any idea is a good idea*
Brainstorm the following:

- What do you stand for?
- What are you often complimented on?
- What are your core values – what really resonates with you?
- How do you go about your life?
- What's your favourite topic of conversation?
- What do you want to achieve?
- What do you discuss with great enthusiasm?
- What are your strengths?
- What makes you awesome?
- What three things make you memorable?

+ *Bring it all together now*
Now bring all your answers and brainstorming together to create your personal elevator pitch. Make it short and sweet, ideally around thirty seconds, and ensure that the tone and language you use resonate with you. This is not about writing as though you are in someone else's shoes or what you think your

pitch should sound like. If in doubt, check in with your body to see how well the ideas sit with you. If you feel tension in your stomach, trust your gut (2.5) and revise it; change the parts you don't like. Nothing is set in stone.

Read over it and imagine you are another person listening so you can hear yourself back. What do you notice? Does it sound genuine? Do you believe it? Is it the truth?

+ *Remember, remember*
Put the key elements or the whole thing somewhere you can see it to remind you on a daily basis, such as in your wallet. Can you think of an object, such as a coin or a little figurine, that would serve as a good reminder?

Then start pitching to yourself, as practice makes perfect. Make it seamless so you are crystal-clear on what *you* stand for and what you represent. If you want to challenge yourself, then recite it or speak out the main themes in front of the mirror. Stand tall, with both feet fully grounded on the floor, then take a deep breath and speak it out. And be proud.

My Experience

I find this concept quite hard and continue to work on it. I can put together ideas and thoughts from brainstorming, but I struggle to put them into a full-bodied pitch that sums it all up. I think of this like GCSE maths, when you still get points for the workings out, even if the final answer is incomplete or incorrect. This mindset may help you too as you start out. I'm sure that I will get there one day and be able to deliver it fully. Regardless, the process and the concept in its entirety helps my anxiety take a back seat as I remind myself of what I can do well.

Go for It

If you believe it, so will others. Let this be a chance to sell yourself.

9.4 Dream Big

Start small, think big. ... Think about not just tomorrow, but the future. Put a ding in the universe.
– Steve Jobs

Snapshot

It is important to clarify our goals and think ahead to where we want to be. When we feel anxious, things become foggy and we are unable to see the big picture. In these moments, it is helpful to step back and take stock of where we are to reconnect with our overarching goals. Clarity is key in helping us to focus on where we want to get to, so the clearer we make our goals, the easier they are to work towards. When clarifying our goals, we should dream big! If we make it even bigger and better than we can imagine, then the impossible becomes possible.

Absolutely our goals can change over time, but overall, goals act as flags in the sand. It doesn't matter where we have been, or where we are now; what matters is where we want to go. Having a target will make sure that we stay on track. Our lives are too valuable to assume that it will all magically pan out exactly the way we want. Instead, we need to work at it.

As you dream big, make sure you define *your* goals, not someone else's. Borrowed dreams are never strived for in the same way that we would look to achieve our own goals.

Importance to GP'ers

Seeing clearly allows us to move forward with purpose and in a self-assured manner. We can map out our route and know with confidence where we are headed. Complete clarity will ensure that we are not wasting time with distractions, and therefore we can achieve what we want quicker. Obviously, we need an element of flexibility to try a different approach if plans change or if we are not getting the results we want.

Our daily routines bog us down, so we don't find the time to pause, reflect and reconnect with our goals. Therefore, our goals often get waylaid, slipping lower and lower down our priority list. So we need something to aim for. This also gets us to question whether our activities *now* are in line with our overarching goals. Do they all help lead us to what we have set our sights on? If they do not, then we might need to revisit them.

Knowing what fires us up, as well as where we are heading, is invaluable. It leaves us feeling inspired and energised. By connecting to our dreams and goals, our everyday anxiety ebbs away. A clear goal means we can stay on course to go and achieve what we want.

Jump into Action

+ *Dream big*

Write down what you truly want to achieve. What are your goals and aspirations? Think about them as if nothing was holding you back. Question, in your wildest dreams: What do you want to do? What do you really want? Dream big!

Get them all down on paper regardless of how unrealistic they might seem. Have fun. Make sure that all your ideas are clear and positive. Rather than saying, 'I don't want to feel anxious,' instead say, 'I am confident and happy.' This will ensure that they are relatable and easy to access.

+ *Do a reality check*
Where are you currently in relation to these goals? How will you
know when you have achieved one?

Write down what the benefits would be if you were to achieve
these goals. Get curious about what you write down and what it
will give you if you carry it out and succeed.

+ *Practise the power of three*
After you reflect on where you are with achieving these goals,
use the same format from chapter 6.4, *Wheel of Life*, to rate them
out of 10, with 0 representing not achieved at all and 10 being
these dreams are fully realised. Just pop down a gut feeling. Do
not put much thought into it.

Having rated your goals on where you are currently, write
down what would make each a 10. Question what feelings,
emotions and activities would have to be achieved for you to
fully reach your goal. Who would you be? What would you
stand for?

Now write down three actions you can take this week to
ensure you are advancing towards your goals. Make them
realistic but challenging.

+ *Set short-term goals*
Ask yourself the following questions to help you set short-term
goals:

- What do you want to achieve?
- How will you know when you have it?
- How will you feel?
- Have you done anything recently to help you achieve this
  dream?
- What worked and what didn't?
- What is the gap between where you are now and where
  you want to be?

- What could be your first step?

+ *Imagine future you*
Form a clear image of who you want to be five years from now
What will you look like? Who will you be? What will you stand
for? How will you carry yourself? What will be important to
you? What responsibility will you have across your personal life
and work life? What will you be proud of? What knowledge do
you have in the future? What do you want to tell your current
self? What advice do you want to give your current self? What
could you start doing differently now?

My Experience

I love thinking big and long term! If ever I am feeling anxious
and out of control, I find relief by sitting down and clarifying
my goals. I'm often more stressed when I am disconnected either
because I don't know where I am heading or I am doing things
that are too far off track and don't fit in with the bigger picture.
Dreaming big brings me back to centre and leaves me feeling
more confident. I also find that the bigger and better I make the
goals, my brain automatically gets on board to try to achieve
them, however crazy they might seem.

Where there is a will, there is a way, but we always need to
know what the will is. As I've mentioned, I am a doer, so there is
no struggle for me to put plans into action. As my dreams become
reality, I feel proud that I have taken the time to understand
where I am heading, and therefore I acknowledge the effort it
has taken once I have got there. And then, of course, I celebrate!

Go for It

Begin to make your goals a reality by starting today. 'Now' is
the magic word when it comes to achieving your goals – the only
way to get there quickly is to jump into action right now.

Conclusion: The Last Word (for Now ...)

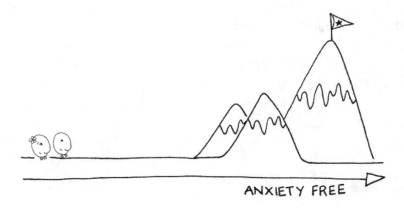

ANXIETY FREE

I hope that you have found at least one thing helpful in this book to give you a breather from your anxiety. My wish for you is that you keep returning to this book to cement these habits and continue to make new ones. Therefore building an ever-expanding wealth of resources to help you manage your anxiety better. My hope is that you will live the life you want, a life where anything is possible.

Good luck to you.

Agi

P.S. Remember what Dr. Seuss says in *Oh, the Places You'll Go!*:

You're off to Great Places!
Today is your day!
Your mountain is waiting.
So ... *get on your way!*

Thank Yous

My deepest thanks go to everyone who has helped me to pull this book together. I got in the way of myself, and so it has been a bit of a journey to getting this completed. Thank you to everyone who believed in me to finish this book. And thank you to Millie Baring for bringing George and Polly, the two characters of Generation Panic, to life.

Thank you to my family, who are an ongoing support to me and just incredible – they have accepted all the parts of me.

Thank you to my dearest Lola, who brings pure joy and laughter to our lives and reminds me to take everything lightly.

And finally, but most importantly, to my husband, Gautam. I cannot thank him enough for being my Safe Person, picking me up when down and always seeing the best in me. None of this – where I am today and the world that I have – would have been at all possible without him. I felt lucky when I met him and still do today.

BOOKS

SPIRITUALITY

O is a symbol of the world, of oneness and unity; this eye represents knowledge and insight. We publish titles on general spirituality and living a spiritual life. We aim to inform and help you on your own journey in this life.
If you have enjoyed this book, why not tell other readers by posting a review on your preferred book site?
Recent bestsellers from O-Books are:

Heart of Tantric Sex

Diana Richardson
Revealing Eastern secrets of deep love and intimacy to Western couples.
Paperback: 978-1-90381-637-0 ebook: 978-1-84694-637-0

Crystal Prescriptions

The A-Z guide to over 1,200 symptoms and their healing crystals
Judy Hall
The first in the popular series of eight books, this handy little guide is packed as tight as a pill-bottle with crystal remedies for ailments.
Paperback: 978-1-90504-740-6 ebook: 978-1-84694-629-5

Take Me To Truth
Undoing the Ego
Nouk Sanchez, Tomas Vieira
The best-selling step-by-step book on shedding the Ego, using the
teachings of *A Course In Miracles*.
Paperback: 978-1-84694-050-7 ebook: 978-1-84694-654-7

The 7 Myths about Love...Actually!
The Journey from your HEAD to the HEART of your SOUL
Mike George
Smashes all the myths about LOVE.
Paperback: 978-1-84694-288-4 ebook: 978-1-84694-682-0

The Holy Spirit's Interpretation of the New Testament
A Course in Understanding and Acceptance
Regina Dawn Akers
Following on from the strength of *A Course In Miracles*, NTI
teaches us how to experience the love and oneness of God.
Paperback: 978-1-84694-085-9 ebook: 978-1-78099-083-5

The Message of A Course In Miracles
A translation of the Text in plain language
Elizabeth A. Cronkhite
A translation of *A Course in Miracles* into plain, everyday
language for anyone seeking inner peace. The companion
volume, *Practicing A Course In Miracles*, offers practical lessons
and mentoring.
Paperback: 978-1-84694-319-5 ebook: 978-1-84694-642-4

Your Simple Path
Find Happiness in every step
Ian Tucker
A guide to helping us reconnect with what is really important in our lives.
Paperback: 978-1-78279-349-6 ebook: 978-1-78279-348-9

365 Days of Wisdom
Daily Messages To Inspire You Through The Year
Dadi Janki
Daily messages which cool the mind, warm the heart and guide you along your journey.
Paperback: 978-1-84694-863-3 ebook: 978-1-84694-864-0

Body of Wisdom
Women's Spiritual Power and How it Serves
Hilary Hart
Bringing together the dreams and experiences of women across the world with today's most visionary spiritual teachers.
Paperback: 978-1-78099-696-7 ebook: 978-1-78099-695-0

Dying to Be Free
From Enforced Secrecy to Near Death to True Transformation
Hannah Robinson
After an unexpected accident and near-death experience, Hannah Robinson found herself radically transforming her life, while a remarkable new insight altered her relationship with her father, a practising Catholic priest.
Paperback: 978-1-78535-254-6 ebook: 978-1-78535-255-3

The Ecology of the Soul
A Manual of Peace, Power and Personal Growth for Real People
in the Real World
Aidan Walker
Balance your own inner Ecology of the Soul to regain your
natural state of peace, power and wellbeing.
Paperback: 978-1-78279-850-7 ebook: 978-1-78279-849-1

Not I, Not other than I
The Life and Teachings of Russel Williams
Steve Taylor, Russel Williams
The miraculous life and inspiring teachings of one of the World's
greatest living Sages.
Paperback: 978-1-78279-729-6 ebook: 978-1-78279-728-9

On the Other Side of Love
A woman's unconventional journey towards wisdom
Muriel Maufroy
When life has lost all meaning, what do you do?
Paperback: 978-1-78535-281-2 ebook: 978-1-78535-282-9

Practicing A Course In Miracles
A translation of the Workbook in plain language, with mentor's
notes
Elizabeth A. Cronkhite
The practical second and third volumes of The Plain-Language
A Course In Miracles.
Paperback: 978-1-84694-403-1 ebook: 978-1-78099-072-9

Quantum Bliss
The Quantum Mechanics of Happiness, Abundance, and Health
George S. Mentz
Quantum Bliss is the breakthrough summary of success and
spirituality secrets that customers have been waiting for.
Paperback: 978-1-78535-203-4 ebook: 978-1-78535-204-1

The Upside Down Mountain
Mags MacKean
A must-read for anyone weary of chasing success and happiness
– one woman's inspirational journey swapping the uphill slog for
the downhill slope.
Paperback: 978-1-78535-171-6 ebook: 978-1-78535-172-3

Your Personal Tuning Fork
The Endocrine System
Deborah Bates
Discover your body's health secret, the endocrine system, and
'twang' your way to sustainable health!
Paperback: 978-1-84694-503-8 ebook: 978-1-78099-697-4

Readers of ebooks can buy or view any of these bestsellers by
clicking on the live link in the title. Most titles are published
in paperback and as an ebook. Paperbacks are available in
traditional bookshops. Both print and ebook formats are
available online.

Find more titles and sign up to our readers' newsletter at
http://www.johnhuntpublishing.com/mind-body-spirit

Follow us on Facebook at https://www.facebook.com/OBooks/
and Twitter at https://twitter.com/obooks